P9-CBT-519

In a culture that spends its days killing time, wasting time, or managing time, John Perritt urges us to become intentional about how we number our days. He does so not from a sense of guilt or manipulation, but from a rich Gospel basis: Jesus Christ has redeemed us, everything about us, including the very minutes of our days spent well or poorly. In gratitude to him, we use 'all our days and all our hours' for his glory–not in an attempt to gain his favor or in a rigorous dutiful attempt to burn ourselves out, but in response to the wonder that the King of Kings deigns to call us his beloved and let us rest beneath his wings. Here is true wisdom for numbering our days.

Sean Michael Lucas
Senior Minister, First Presbyterian Church, Hattiesburg, Mississippi
Associate Professor of Church History,
Reformed Theological Seminary, Jackson, Mississippi

I'm grateful to John Perritt for offering so much wise and godly counsel in this book. He challenged me to consider my priorities so I can love God and love my neighbors with all my heart, soul, mind, and strength. No doubt he'll do the same for you.

Collin Hansen
Editorial director of The Gospel Coalition and author of
Blind Spots: Becoming a Courageous, Compassionate, and Commissioned Church

As soon as one becomes a disciple of Jesus Christ they quickly realize that there are some things about their lives that they must change right away. One of those things is how we spend our time so that it reflects how God wants us spending our time wisely. God has called all of His followers to redeem their time. In a day and age when everyone wants to tell you how *busy* they are or how they don't have enough *time,* John Perritt gets right to the heart of the matter and tells you exactly how you ought to be disciplined with your time. This book is ruthlessly practical. I heartedly recommend it to the disciple who desires to honor the Lord with their days.

Wilson A. Shirley
Senior Pastor, Cornerstone Presbyterian Church, Huntsville, Alabama

Time management is a struggle into which most of us are locked on a daily basis. For some, our predilection for control makes us incapable of flexibility and robs us of joy. For others, our inability to plan and execute consistently sows the seeds of chaos and pushes the eternal to the margins in favor of the temporary, and the urgent is too often prioritized over the important. Thinking Christianly about how we spend our time therefore presents a daunting challenge, but *Your Days Are Numbered* succeeds in addressing it with simplicity and practicality. If heeded, John Perritt's common sense proposals grounded in scriptural principle will enable us to 'redeem the time'. My own conscience was stirred as I read, and I have already made changes in my own life as a result. This is a useful volume.

David Strain
Senior Minister, First Presbyterian Church, Jackson, Mississippi

Of all the gifts God gives to us, few are more precious and few are more fleeting than the gift of time. Your days are numbered and you are responsible to faithfully steward each one of them for the good of others and the glory of God. This book will teach and encourage you to make the most of the time God gives you.

Tim Challies
Blogger at www.challies.com

I loved it. I believe most everyone *knows* that busyness, bad time management, poor time stewardship, are a problem. But I think a small handful are aware of the depth and severity of the problem. Nor do they have any 'tools' in their tool belt to know how to fix it. This book gives us tools.

The author did us all a favor by starting with the gospel. He gave us the hope of God's eternal solution to our wasting of days and then you kept the gospel in front as God's solution for redeeming the days.

I was inspired to *'Be very careful, then, how you live—not as unwise but as wise, making the most of every opportunity.'* I have been chewing on this constantly. It's worth the price of the book alone.

His gave me questions to ask as I think about how to become a good steward of the numbered days God has given.

In other words this book is not just inspiring, it is instructional. People have NO IDEA how to navigate time in the 21st century. They need guidance and John Perritt gives that to them.

David McNeely
Director of Young Families and Adults Pastor,
Perimeter Church,, Johns Creek, Georgia

To: Jonathan & Kim
Love, Mom & Dad
2016

JOHN
PERRITT

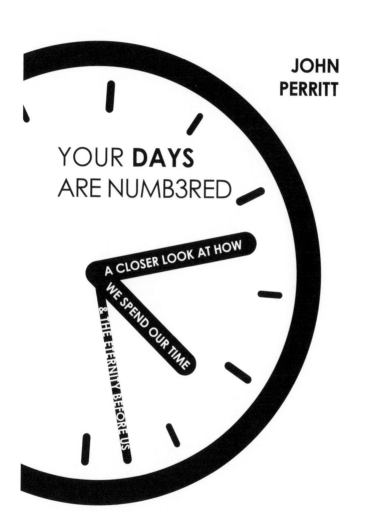

YOUR **DAYS**
ARE NUMB3RED

A CLOSER LOOK AT HOW

WE SPEND OUR TIME

& THE ETERNITY BEFORE US

CHRISTIAN
FOCUS

Scripture quotations are from *The Holy Bible, English Standard Version*, copyright © 2001 by Crossway Bibles, a division of Good News Publishers. Used by permission. All rights reserved.

John Perritt is the Youth Director at Pear Orchard Presbyterian Church in Ridgeland, Mississippi. He has served in youth ministry for over a decade. He has published articles for The Gospel Coalition and Reformation 21. He occasionally blogs on film and theology at www.reelthinking.us. He and his wife, Ashleigh, have four children.

Copyright © John Perritt 2016

paperback ISBN 978-1-78191-744-2
epub ISBN 978-1-78191-789-3
Mobi ISBN 978-1-78191-790-9

10 9 8 7 6 5 4 3 2 1

Published in 2016
by
Christian Focus Publications Ltd,
Geanies House, Fearn, Ross-shire,
IV20 1TW, Great Britain.

www.christianfocus.com

Cover Designer
Pete Barnsley, Creative Hoot

Printed and bound
by
Bell & Bain, Glasgow

All rights reserved. No part of this publication may be reproduced, stored in a retrieval system, or transmitted, in any form, by any means, electronic, mechanical, photocopying, recording or otherwise without the prior permission of the publisher or a licence permitting restricted copying. In the U.K. such licences are issued by the Copyright Licensing Agency, Saffron House, 6-10 Kirby Street, London, EC1 8TS www.cla.co.uk

CONTENTS

Foreword **9**

Introduction **11**

1 The sure foundation **15**

Section 1
What our days are made of

2 Time **23**

3 Hobbies **29**

4 Trivial pursuits: Temporal versus eternal **39**

5 Busyness: No time for God **51**

6 The mundane **57**

Section 2
Biblical practices that assist our days

7 A word (or two) on stewardship **65**

8 Sabbath rest **71**

Section 3
Practically numbering your days

9 How many days do you have left?
    How to order the time we have **89**

10 Twenty-four hours and non-negotiables **109**

11 Some needed disciplines **127**

12 God is God and you're not **135**

13 Conclusion **143**

Appendix 1 – A charge to men **147**

Appendix 2 – Ten good Christian books to read **155**

Further reading **159**

FOREWORD

IN an age awash with concern for leisure, what are Bible-focused Christians to do? This generation, perhaps more than any before it, needs wise counsel to use time and energy in ways that bring God glory. John Perritt has given a great deal of energy into thinking through the issues raised by today's culture and what he has written here deserves our attention.

Avoiding over-spiritualization and the problems that come from a distorted view of creation, Perritt expertly guides us through the difficulties. He will be too lenient for some; too demanding of others but this only shows the careful navigation he undertakes in addressing matters that raise our passions. This is essential reading for those concerned with addressing the question, 'How may I glorify God in the legitimate pursuit of leisure?' I heartily recommend it.

Derek W. H. Thomas

Senior Minister, First Presbyterian Church, Columbia South Carolina
Robert Strong Professor of Systematic and Pastoral Theology,
Reformed Theological Seminary, Atlanta, Georgia

*This book is dedicated to
my loving wife and children.
Apart from my salvation,
you are the greatest graces bestowed in my life.*

INTRODUCTION

*So teach us to number our days that we
may get a heart of wisdom.*
Psalm 90:12

WHEN I was in seminary I took a class entitled *Leadership*. One of our first assignments for the class was to log all of our everyday activities in thirty-minute increments. That is, if you brushed your teeth, took a shower and got dressed in thirty minutes, you were to log that down. If you spent thirty minutes on your commute, you were to write that down. We were supposed to log something every thirty-minutes for two weeks.

Two things became apparent from this assignment. First, I became keenly aware of the way in which I spent my time, and second, I became keenly aware of the fact that I wasted much of it. The resonating influence this exercise had on me makes me think it might not be a bad exercise for you. Why not give it a try? It may prove to be truly helpful.

Wasting time might not seem like a big deal to some, except for the fact that our time really isn't ours, but God's. Not only that, but it is a limited resource. You can be the richest person in the world and you still can't buy more time. The reality is, there is a clock ticking somewhere, right now, and it is the clock of your life. Seconds that add into minutes, which add into hours, which add into days are ticking off your life.

It is a sobering reality to think that this may be the last book you read. This may be your last day on earth. You have plans today, tomorrow, and the years to come, but those may never be realised. Many of us know this reality, but we *never* think that it will be us. The truth is, it very well could be. Why wouldn't it be you? What makes you so confident it won't be you?

Now, you can let this reality frighten you or depress you, but that isn't the biblical perspective we should have on this topic; plus that isn't the purpose of this book. Rather, let the reality of death and eternity with a limited amount of time on this earth, spur you on to good works for the glory of God. Use the limited amount of time that Christ purchased to point others to His Kingdom.

When we think of major issues facing the church today, the way in which we spend our time might not seem like the best topic to waste our … time on. However, when I think of some major issues like depression, suicide, substance abuse, adultery, fornication, pornography, eating disorders, divorce, teenage drinking, evangelism, discipleship, service, the list can go on and on, I see one commonality between these vast topics. It is that they are all affected by our use of time.

We will look at some of these topics in greater detail as we get into the book, but I would like to posit this thought. Maybe the way in which we steward the time given us is *the* major problem with Christians today. Just maybe if we spent our time a bit differently from the rest of the world, issues like divorce, suicide, drug abuse, porn addiction, and others, would start to be less of a problem. However, when you look at the way most Christians spend God's time, it really isn't very different from the ways in which unbelievers spend their time. It does vary, but it's also very similar. As we go forward, this book will hopefully challenge you to make some drastic changes in the way we abuse the days God has graciously given us.

In Psalm 90 Moses equates wisdom with having a mind-set of numbered days. We all know that our days will end on this earth. Whether that is before Christ returns or not, our earthly days have a limit. Therefore, living with a sense of urgency is a must if we hope to live wisely.

Urgency can cause anxiety in some, but that is not the intent of the psalmist. Rather, we must live with an excitement to make God known. Using our numbered days to spread the good news of Jesus Christ, is time wisely spent. However, the ways in which the average Christian spends their days seems to imply that they will live forever. There's little urgency. The focus is very earthly, not eternal.

This book was written to shift our focus.

If we want a heart of wisdom, according to the psalmist, we must number our days. This book will take a biblical look at the way in which we spend our days to cultivate this mind-set of seeing each day as a vital opportunity to live for the glory of God. James 4:14b says, *'For you are a mist that appears for a little time and then vanishes.'* We have very little time before we vanish, so let's not waste any more of it. Let's get wise and start numbering our days. But first, we must keep a foundational truth before us.

1 THE SURE FOUNDATION

NOT too long ago I was on a youth mission trip to Brazil. One particular day we were doing some work on a drug rehabilitation center. As we were getting a tour of the facility we noticed a clock on the wall that had a phrase written in Portuguese. The men we were working with told us the phrase read, 'Redeem the time you have lost'. This was a powerful thought. The men in the facility had, most likely, forfeited much of their life in the service of their false god of drug addiction. I'm sure they had sacrificed friends, family, possibly wives and children in the pursuit of this false god.

I could not imagine the sense of guilt these men carried around. This was a Christian rehab center, so they are told about the gospel and are assisted in a mighty way to get back to a sense of normalcy. However, the thought of 'redeeming the time you lost' could be a demoralizing thought.

Please know that I in no way intend to question the intentions of the men who serve the facility. They are great men who serve in difficult circumstances which many of us could only imagine. My thought on the phrase is I'm so glad *I* don't have to redeem the time I've lost. Don't get me wrong. There are wise ways we can spend our time and foolish ways we spend our time, and this book hopes to assist us in determining how to prioritize that time. However, if it was up to each of us to redeem our own time, we would be in trouble.

The truth is, Jesus Christ redeemed our time. There wasn't one second of His time on earth that was wasted. The thirty-three years He walked the face of this earth were lived in perfect obedience; therefore, by faith in His finished work every child of God is seen as walking in perfect obedience. Let's think about this a bit more specifically. Since our time affects everything, and each part of your day can be broken up into thoughts, words, and deeds, let's begin there.

Thoughts

What if we could take a video of your mind for the past week or month. And what if you showed up to worship on Sunday morning and the pastor stood up and informed you that they were about to show that video. How would you react? Most would sprint to the front of the sanctuary and tackle the projector to the ground to ensure others didn't see it. Could you imagine the filth people would see? The relationships that would be injured? It would be horrifying.

Jesus Christ walked the face of this earth and never thought a sinful thought. He never lustfully thought about a woman. He never sinfully judged another human being. He never thought hateful thoughts about those He knew would nail Him to the cross. And He never allowed His brain to lazily drift off into worthless day-dreaming.

His mind fully and continually thought about His Father's will. He thought righteous, loving and just thoughts His entire existence. By faith in Jesus, your thoughts are redeemed!

Words

Jesus Christ also never spoke a sinful word. Think about our words and how often we use them. We wake up speaking, texting and emailing. We talk to our television sets as we watch the news or sports. We talk (yell) at drivers behind the safety of our wheel. We talk about people in our minds (see above). We spend a lot of time using spoken or written words. In fact, our words take up a very significant portion of each day. It's a sobering thought to know that we are going to have to give an account for every word we've ever spoken. Every word? Every word (Matt. 12:36).

Not to worry. If you have faith in Christ, He has redeemed your words. Yes we should strive to speak edifying words to each other and be cautious of the words we speak to our television sets. But by the power of the Holy Spirit, Christ has redeemed your words. All the time you've spent on careless words are redeemed by faith in Him.

Deeds

Confession time. When I was younger, I despised manual labor. I loathed mowing the lawn and would do just about anything to get out of doing it. Acting out of this hatred, when I was in high school, I broke the string on the crank pull to get out of mowing the lawn. Our lawn mower was very old so the string was quite worn, but I assisted its waning strength that day.

Even though I acted out of hatred towards the lawn mower, I really broke it because I was lazy. My laziness superseded my parents' honor. Think of how often we are lazy with our time. Our deeds are tainted with laziness, and quite often, selfishness. More often than not we are the center of our universe, so we spend our time in the way we want to spend it.

Because of this we serve self and not others. We are prone to avoid serving and hospitality because those things are never truly convenient. And, if they are convenient some may question if they're truly service. Isn't service, by definition, inconvenient? We sin by deeds of omission (things I should have done but didn't) and deeds of commission (things I did but shouldn't have done) every day.

This again should help us to see how faithful our Savior was. Jesus never spent a lazy second in His life. Jesus never avoided service towards others. Jesus' deeds were always perfectly righteous and it was those deeds that have purchased our righteous robe. By faith in Jesus, all your deeds are now righteous!

The Greatest Commandment

You shall love the Lord your God with all your heart and with all your soul and with all your mind. MATTHEW 22:37

And all of these above issues really come back to the Greatest Commandment. Loving God the Father. Jesus Christ loved His Father more than anyone or anything. Jesus so wanted to do His Father's will that there wasn't a temptation that rose above this.

Where we have many loves towards people and things that are idolatrous, Jesus spent every moment of His life perfectly loving and following His Father. Think about the time you spend on idols. To assist you with this, look at your calendar. What has the most time devoted to it? Whatever that is, chances are that's your idol.

I'm not trying to heap guilt on you, rather I'm illustrating the fact that Jesus perfectly spent His days living for the glory of God so that you, by faith, have perfectly lived for God's glory. As we move forward in this book, the foundational truth of – *Jesus righteously lived every second of His life to redeem your time* – must be at the forefront of your mind. If you lose sight of this truth, you will either live in guilt or self-righteousness. Guilt, because you can't measure up, or self-righteousness because you're going to try and do a bunch of stuff for Jesus. Yes, strive for righteous living, but know that Jesus accomplished that task for you. Your time is *already* redeemed.

TIME TO THINK

✳ Which areas are you already aware of that need work? Which areas of your time do you steward well? Where do you think you'll get offended or defensive? Proceed with a humble heart.

✳ This book is designed to challenge you and question some of the practices of your daily routine. Chances are you may get your toes stepped on. As you proceed, continue to reflect on the finished work of Christ and how your failures will not change the eternity He's secured for His children.

SECTION 1

What our days are made of

2 TIME

WHAT is a day? That could be answered in many different ways, but let's answer this according to time. Every day is made up of a twenty-four-hour period. This is true in any culture all over the world. But, what is time? How would you define it?

In one sense, we could say that time is synonymous with life. We could say time *is* life. We use phrases like *We only have a certain amount of time (life) on this earth*. Or, when mourning the loss of a loved-one we may say, *I wish I could see them just one more time.* Time is life, for it is within the confines of time that our lives exist.

Not only do we see time as valuable when we understand that it encompasses the lives we live, but look at the language we associate with time. If you are doing something that doesn't have much value you might say, *Oh, we didn't do much. Just killed some time.* Killed time?! We know killing can be a bad thing if it isn't in self-defense, so what do we mean by killing time? We are associating life with time. Time possesses life, but we *killed* it.

We know that money is associated with value and we spend a certain amount of it to obtain specific items. If you buy something you may hear someone ask, *How much did that cost? Or, How much would you have to spend to get that?* Cost is counted when we want to purchase an item, but we use the same language when speaking of time. *How much time have you spent with him? I hope it didn't **cost** you too much time.*

So our time has great value attached to it as well as life itself. Why is this? Where does this come from? The beginning.

The first words of the most amazing book ever written (no, not this one) read, *'In the beginning, God …'* (Gen. 1:1a). This tells us that God was and always has been there. He has simply and profoundly existed. He is *eternal.* Eternal is an interesting word, especially when it is being used in a discussion concerning time. As we know, eternality is superior to time, because it is not confined to time.

In verse 26 of the same chapter in Genesis we read, *'Then God said, "Let us make man in our image, after our likeness".'* So, God is eternal and has now made man(kind) after His image and likeness. What does that mean for us? It means we still have eternality hardwired in our DNA.

What is time? Time is a result of the fall. Yes, 'In the beginning' refers to a point in time prior to sin. And, God created the entire earth in the span of six days, so there was morning and evening in this span. But time as we know it came about because of the fall. In Genesis 2:17 God gives Adam and Eve the command to abstain from eating the fruit of the tree of the knowledge of good and evil, and says if they eat it they *shall surely die.* Another word for death is expire. Death implies an end, an end to limitless days that never knew death. In a sense, the eternity Adam and Even knew in the Garden, died. How can eternity die?

God told Adam and Eve once they ate of the tree they would die, so did they? No and yes. One might think they would have dropped dead at the first bite because of God's command, but they didn't. Their death is a slow one, a death that is played out over a period of time. This is a death each of us must experience if the Lord doesn't return first. So Adam and Eve did not receive an instantaneous death, rather, the creation of time was ushered in. They now had a limit to their days. They would expire. They would run out of time before returning back to the eternal state. Therefore, their eternality, given to them by God, has been delayed. This is true of every individual on earth.

We are all eternal beings who have entered into time, but our time is running out. Our bodies will expire and we will return to the eternity we were designed to live, if we are in Jesus Christ. If you do not have faith in Jesus Christ, there is another eternity that awaits you, one of weeping and gnashing of teeth (Matt. 25:30).

One other aspect of time I want to briefly mention is that it brings about fatigue. In Isaiah 40:28 we read, '*Have you not known? Have you not heard? The LORD is the everlasting God, the Creator of the ends of the earth. He does not faint or grow weary; his understanding is unsearchable.*'

This verse tells us that God is everlasting and one aspect of everlasting-ness is strength. By implication we can say since we aren't everlasting, we are weak. We *do* faint and grow weary, to use the words of the prophet Isaiah. Therefore, time makes us weak and beats us down.

The point is, time is a result of the fall. Time is unnatural to us. We never feel like we have enough time with friends, we never want a great football game to end, we always want to stay up later or get up earlier, there aren't enough hours in the day, you never get on top of work at the office, the kids just grew up too fast, where did the time go? All of these things affirm we are eternal beings who have now been clothed in time and we must learn how to live in its confines. In a sense the old saying is true. Time is against us. We are at war with our time, because time is at war with our eternal natures.

As we move forward we must keep these truths in mind. We were created for an eternity, time came about as a result of the fall, and time is warring against us. This is an important foundation we must have our feet firmly planted on. Remember, there is not one aspect of our day which isn't impacted by our use of time, for time *is* life.

TIME TO THINK

✳ Reflect more on how the fall impacts our time. How does it war against you on most days? At home? At work? In recreation?

✳ Since we were all created with eternity hard-wired in us, how does this affect you on a daily basis? Do you take more on yourself than you're able to handle because of this truth? Are your calendars too full because you fear you will miss out on something?

3 HOBBIES

ACCORDING to my dictionary in Apple's pages, a hobby is defined as *an activity done regularly in one's leisure time for pleasure*. Let's break that definition down for a minute. A hobby is done *regularly*, therefore, it takes up a significant amount of time. Maybe not as much as work or other daily tasks, but hobbies are typically regular things.

The definition also says that they are done in our *leisure time*. Hmmm, leisure time? What is meant by this phrase? Well, we know leisure time is synonymous with free time. However, how much of our time is actually free? We've established that time is synonymous with life and value, so how can we now say that time is free?

The last part of the definition says that a hobby is done for *pleasure*. Christians know there is no such thing as true joy and pleasure outside of God. Therefore, the deeper we strive to find pleasure in God, the deeper the pleasure we receive. So why is it that our hobbies are often in competition with God? I've noticed that what people call hobbies seemingly have very little to do with God. In fact, they often hinder their Christian walk with Him. This does not mean our hobbies can't feed a deeper relationship with God or that some of us have hobbies that are deeply connected to knowing God more. I would say however, that many of us have hobbies that seem to be disconnected from God. Survey your own hobbies, how connected are they to the Eternal One?

Before I get ahead of myself, let's look back at the beginning of that definition, *an activity done regularly …*

Regularity

Our definition of a hobby starts with regularity. And, as I mentioned, some have hobbies that seem to draw them away from God while others have hobbies that can deepen their relationship with God. For example, maybe following a certain sports team is a hobby of yours. For the unbeliever, they only enjoy what is before them. For the Christian, they see another layer to sports. They know the amazing athleticism that they appreciate has been granted by the hand of God. Therefore, they can actually worship God through their hobby. This is why our theology is so important.

Everyone has a theology. As R.C. Sproul says, 'Everyone's a theologian.'[1] That is, everyone on the face of this earth possesses thoughts and beliefs about God. Some believe in Him, some don't and some are indifferent but they all have thoughts about God or a theology of God, because they were created in His image. Romans 1 tells us that the knowledge of God is written on mankind's conscience as well as through all of creation (Rom. 1:18-25).

Part of this knowledge of God, both in our consciences and through creation, moves us to worship. Think back to the hobby of a sports team. We can worship God through that activity or we simply worship creation. This should come as no surprise since the first of the Ten Commandments reads, *'You shall have no other gods before me'* (Exod. 20:3). This being the first and greatest commandment tells us that we are worshipers. We *will* worship.

This first commandment is implying that we will be worshiping other things all the time. This is because we were designed to be worshipers, but now our sin is confusing our worship. Since we are sinners, our understanding of God gets misdirected. We look to money to give us what only God can give us. We look to our spouses/children/friends to give us what only God can give us. We look to hobbies to give us what only God can give us.

---

1. R.C. Sproul, *Everyone's a Theologian*. Reformation Trust Publishing. Lake Mary, Florida (2014).

In Ed Welch's, *Addictions: A Banquet in the Grave*, he points out that 'Addictions are ultimately a disorder of worship.'[2] When we begin worshiping something too much, it becomes an addiction. Now, there are varying levels of addictions, but we can understand the close connections between worship and addiction. This addiction could be *an activity done regularly*; i.e. a hobby. In my experience, I've heard many people refer to things as hobbies which could probably be considered idol worship or addiction.

For example, have you known anyone who has a hobby that's done so regularly that if another person stands in the way of that hobby conflict ensues? Or, maybe you know someone whose hobby completely restructures their entire week? That is, they have to wake up extra early to get a start on this hobby or go to bed much later because they are working on this hobby. Whether they're staying up too late or waking up too early, this is impacting other days in their week. You see, this hobby is *shaping* the rest of their life. It is something they won't allow anyone to get in the way of. Sounds sort of like an addiction, right?

Even if you don't think of your hobbies as idols you are worshiping, be careful! If a hobby is something done regularly it runs the great risk of becoming an idol. The more times you are bowing down to it, the closer it is becoming to your heart.

---

2. Ed Welch, *Addictions*, preface xvi. P&R Publishing. Phillipsburg, New Jersey (November 1, 2001).

This simply happens to anything that becomes regular or habitual.

Here are some helpful questions to ask of your hobby. Is your hobby something you use as an escape? When you feel stressed, tired or angry, do you flee to your hobby? Why does your hobby bring you happiness? This will help you discern if your hobby is something you worship; if it's something that's subtly become a false god to you. The truth for the Christian is that we are to seek refuge in God (Ps. 2:12, 5:11, 7:1). However, our false gods end up becoming a false refuge for us. We run to them to escape stress and find happiness. Often these idols can offer us a temporary refuge, but they will not give us the refuge we need. Therefore, search your heart and see what it reveals about your hobbies.

Free time

Another aspect to the definition of a hobby was that it's something we do in our free time. If you remember, what I said previously about time is that it's not *our* time. Scripture tells us, *'You are not your own, for you were bought with a price. So glorify God in your body'* (1 Cor. 6:19b-20).

Now, these verses were discussing sexual sin and the fact that we cannot do what we want with our bodies. However, the principle here informs us that our very lives don't belong to us. We are not autonomous creatures – we belong/answer to another. Therefore, how should we interpret the term 'free time'? The lives/time Christ bought us wasn't free for Him. Let us reflect on Philippians 2:5-11:

'Have this mind among yourselves which is yours in Christ Jesus, who, though he was in the form of God, did not count equality with God a thing to be grasped, but made himself nothing, taking on the form of a servant, being born in the likeness of men. And being found in human form, he humbled himself by becoming obedient to the point of death, even death on a cross. Therefore, God has highly exalted him and bestowed on him the name that is above every name, so that at the name of Jesus every knee should bow, in heaven and on earth and under the earth, and every tongue confess that Jesus Christ is Lord, to the glory of God the Father.'

What an unmeasurable cost for Jesus Christ! **Free? Free time?!** Jesus Christ left His throne, took on flesh, was misunderstood, hated, mocked, tortured and betrayed for you and for me. What a cost it was to redeem His rebellious children. It certainly wasn't free for Him. Should this give us pause in using the phrase 'free time'?

I know there are times when events or meetings are cancelled and that frees up some time, but Christians must be cautious of throwing around this term. Our lives are not our own and neither is our time. The time we have cost our Savior much, so let us keep that in mind.

Pleasure

Now we get to the last part of the definition. How would you define pleasure? Think of it this way. If you could plan one day to go exactly how you wanted it to go, what would it consist of? What would you like to do? This will help you get closer to defining pleasure.

Our sinful hearts often do a great job of convincing us that God is against our joy. Think back to Adam and Eve. God gave and gave and gave, but they were convinced life was lacking something. They were convinced God was keeping them from something. In a similar way most of us believe church is boring and the world is fun. Service to God's Kingdom results in loss, but service to our kingdoms results in a good time. Let's consider two important verses of Scripture here.

In Hebrews 11:25 we read of Moses *'choosing rather to be mistreated with the people of God than to enjoy the fleeting pleasures of sin.'* This verse tells us many things, but one thing it teaches us is that sin is fun. I have always said, if sin wasn't fun we wouldn't be tempted to indulge it. Sin does bring pleasure, but it's fleeting.

Therefore, our hobbies may bring about pleasure, but if we aren't seeing these earthly pleasures through the lens of Scripture, they are fleeting. They possess a pleasure that will not last.

Another Scripture I want us to look at comes from Luke 9:24, *'For whoever would save his life will lose it, but whoever loses his life for my sake will save it.'* When I was younger I knew this verse was profound, but I didn't really understand it. Basically this verse is telling us that the more we live for selfish pursuits, the more empty our lives will be. That is, we could indulge ourselves in money, possessions, the pursuit of happiness, success and yet ultimately you will – guaranteed, one hundred percent – lose your life.

The movie, *About a Boy*, follows the story of Will Freeman (Hugh Grant) who is an immature man that has lived a life for himself. When Will was young, he had a hit song that brought him fame and fortune and he has exploited that fame and fortune in the pursuit of his kingdom. However, Will Freeman is not a *free-man* at all and has become enslaved to his selfish pursuits. He's become cynical because he has actually experienced so much in life and it has not brought him pleasure. In one particular scene of the film he remarks, *'I had lived a full life, but wasted it.'*

Will is affirming what Jesus Christ said, as well as testifying how many of us live our lives. We try, so hard, to save our lives by filling them with so many things. So many pleasures, but we have full lives that are wasted.

Take a look at your hobbies. Look at the things you do on a regular basis. Are they feeble attempts to save our lives and give us earthly (fleeting) pleasures? The interesting promise we have from Luke is that when we lose our lives in the world's eyes, we actually get more fulfilment. Isn't that the way God always works? He works backwards from the world. If you give, you receive. If you lose, you find.

God does not rob our joy, He redefines it. He gives us a deeper, fuller joy when our pleasure is rooted in Him. Are your hobbies, or regular activities, lived with this mind-set? I see many a hobby that pulls people away from Lord's Day worship and service. Many a hobby that wears people down, so they're physically present on Sundays but spiritually absent.

So what am I saying? I am not saying quit all of your hobbies, but I am asking you to evaluate them. Are your hobbies in competition with the Lord's Kingdom? Are they keeping you from serving your church and others? Are they selfish pursuits of your own pleasure? Do they rob your family of significant time? Do they draw you closer to the Lord and make you a more significant servant for His Kingdom?

Let me give you a personal example. For starters, I don't have this figured out by any means. One hobby I enjoy is movies. I've seen a lot of movies in my lifetime, but it wasn't until recently that I started watching them from a biblical perspective. I look back on my life and think of the time I've wasted watching movies. There have been times I've looked to movies to fill the void in my heart. I've used them merely as an escape. A selfish means to give me what I want.

However, I saw emptiness time and time again from film. My hobby failed me. However, now that I have begun to engage my mind a bit more and consider film through the lens of Scripture, I've found more enjoyment from the hobby. It actually fails me less and I end up being blessed by this approach. I've also refused to watch some movies, not simply because of the content, but because of the time it would cost. I realized I had a limited amount and I didn't want to spend it on that particular movie.

Please do not hear me propagating a karma-ish theology. What I am affirming is what Luke said. I became more aware of using film for my selfish pleasure and started viewing it Scripturally and God actually did what He said He would. I enjoy movies more when I use them for my glory less. Apply this to your hobbies. See them as a means to teach you more about the Lord. If you discover that your hobby is in fact in competition with God, maybe it's time for a new hobby.

TIME TO THINK

✳ How did this chapter redefine your hobbies? Do you see some of you hobbies as idols?

✳ What do you think about the notion of 'free time'? Do you think Christ's finished work will have an impact on the next available 'free time' that comes across your path?

✳ What do you typically run to for pleasure? Why is it that our hearts are typically drawn to temporal things when we have 'free time'? What does that reveal about our hearts?

4 TRIVIAL PURSUITS – TEMPORAL VERSUS ETERNAL

A WHILE back I was reading John Piper's *A Sweet and Bitter Providence: Sex, Race, and the Sovereignty of God*. It is a collection of sermons from the book of Ruth and Piper said something that really resonated with me.

> *'One of the greatest diseases of our day is trifling. The things with which most people spend most of their time are trivial. And what makes this a disease is that we were meant to live for magnificent causes. None of us is really content with trivial pursuits of the world. Our souls will not be satisfied with trifles. Why is there a whole section of the newspaper devoted to sports and almost nothing devoted to the greatest story in the universe – the growth*

and spread of the church of Jesus Christ? It is madness that insignificant games should occupy such a central role in our culture compared to the work of God in Christ.'[1]

Piper really hits on something. We trifle our days away. If you were to step back and look at how you spent your 'free' time, much of it would be spent on worthless trivialities. Guess what? Satan doesn't want you to think about that. The truth is, most of the ways we waste our time are on 'innocent' things. While Twitter and Facebook shouldn't necessarily be classified as 'innocent', much of what people do could be classified as such. However, to reference Piper again, he once sent a tweet that provides a helpful perspective, 'One of the great uses of Twitter and Facebook will be to prove at the Last Day that prayerlessness was not from lack of time.' Innocently spending time on Twitter and Facebook (and Vine and Instagram and 'insert your favourite social media here') can do some harm to our prayer life, which can feed a lifestyle that's anything but innocent. Innocent things often become deadly in the hands of our Enemy.

The point of this chapter is to cultivate an eternal perspective. I want us to look at our activities in the light of eternity. Think of the typical death-bed testimony of someone who's realized they wasted their life. *I wish I had spent more time …*

---

1. John Piper, *A Sweet and Bitter Providence: Sex, Race and the Sovereignty of God*, p. 120. Crossway. Wheaton, Illinois (2010).

When we look at our typical activities in light of an eternity, it gives us some great perspective. Although I know this chapter may be a tough pill to swallow, the exhortation is a loving one.

Open your eyes

The New Testament continuously charges us to take our eyes away from this world and focus on the life to come. From Paul's second letter to the church in Corinth we read this exhortation, *'as we look not to the things that are seen but to the things that are unseen. For the things that are seen are transient, but the things that are unseen are eternal'* (2 Cor. 4:18). If God's objective is to have our focus on the eternal, I guarantee you Satan's objective is to keep our sights set on the temporal. And he does that with excellence.

Let us consider beauty for a moment. What is beauty? When I even mention that word, I'm pretty certain that most of you thought about external beauty. Modern culture has so perverted our definition of beauty that we have people who are suicidal and depressed because the world's definition doesn't describe them. Eating disorders are being found among ten to twelve-year-olds because the world says you must be a certain dress size to be beautiful.

Women and men go to great lengths to be tan, even though they know they will most likely get cancer from the source that makes them tanner. It is because Satan has fed us the lie that the external is what matters. He has long gotten our minds off the eternal and makes us focus on the temporal. This is not to say that we cannot enjoy or celebrate external beauty. There are physically beautiful people mentioned in Scripture (2 Sam. 14:25; Esther 2:7) but there's a greater depth to beauty than what the eyes can behold.

If you were to stop and think about the time and money we spend on the temporal, it is quite sobering. Please be patient with me, the next example ventures into some sacred ground, but hear me out.

Football, both European and American, are fun recreational events. Not only can fans cheer on uniquely gifted athletes, but the fellowship with other fans makes sporting events an enjoyable occasion that fosters biblical fellowship. Christians not only have the freedom to enjoy various athletic events, but should seek to experience these at some point in their lives. That being said, think of the amount of time that is given over to these sporting events. Many of them are an all-day occasion. Travel to the game, celebration and anticipation before the game, actually experiencing the game, celebration (or depression) after the game and more fellowship. These events easily dominate an entire day in our lives.

I'm trying to 'tip-toe' here because we can quickly slip into a legalistic tone if we are not careful. But the point of this book is to get you to wrestle with your use of time; therefore, just consider this. If you are a person that follows a certain team's entire season, doesn't miss a game, and spends twelve to fifteen hours on your team at weekends, but doesn't give twelve to fifteen hours to your Savior on His day (i.e., the Sabbath), or in the service of God's church, you may want to be more discerning with your time. Ask yourself this question. Have I ever given twelve to fifteen hours in the service of the Lord? If I have, how often? Am I reluctant to? Why is my heart continually happy to give this large amount of time to a sports team, but not to the Lover of my soul?

Another way to think about it is to consider a specific issue, like abortion. Most Christians are pro-life, but, as a friend of mine asked me, 'What are we actually *doing* to show we are against abortion?' That really convicted me. Yes I am against abortion but what do I do to stop the killing of babies besides praying (sometimes, if I remember) and just feeling bad about the reality of abortion?

Think of this issue in regards to the videos that exposed the barbaric practices of Planned Parenthood. Planned Parenthood is a women's health organization that's the leading abortion industry in the United States. Videos were released exposing the fact that PP offices were being compensated from the selling of infant body parts. There was outrage and discussion that occurred over social media, but how many pro-life Christians were moved to action to stop this? How many actually exerted any effort against Planned Parenthood?

As of now, the angst has died down. I can almost guarantee you that a major factor that this short-lived concern was extinguished was because of busyness. Christians are too consumed with other things.

The reason I bring up the issue of abortion when talking about the time given to athletic events is to ask this question. Could you imagine if all the Christians across the world spent the time and money they spend following an athletic team, and poured that into efforts to stop abortion? Imagine that, twelve to fifteen hours a week in the pursuit of rescuing the lives of unborn infants. Giving time for the unborn? Or our football teams? I'm not saying there has to be an 'either or' here, I'm just saying that one issue is trivial and one is eternal.

Ultimate joy

I first heard of comedian Brian Regan in 1997 and he is still one of my favourite comedians. He does a bit about pop tarts and remarks that there are microwave directions on the actual box of pop tarts. The cooking time for the microwave is a total of three seconds. He exclaims, 'If your day requires you zap-frying your pop-tarts, you might want to loosen up your schedule.' Using Regan's wisdom, we too may want to loosen our schedules a bit.

Sadly Satan has convinced us to focus on what is seen and he has also gotten us to buy the lie that God is against our joy. He has convinced you that if you really want to serve and please God, you must do a bunch of boring things. To make God really happy, you must be miserable. Matt Chandler articulates this well:

'God is the author of every good thing. Pleasure, partying, gardens, work, money, material things, and sex are all his ideas. Adam and Eve were created and set in a garden wearing nothing. That's a great deal! I love the way God started the whole thing: one man, one woman, a bunch of acreage, and naked. "Go, play, frolic, and have a good time." This is what shalom looked like! Somehow we have received the idea that God is a cosmic killjoy, but we stand on Scripture to say that this deep longing in the core of who we are that cries out for happiness and delight was put there by him and he means for us to be satisfied.'[2]

You see, God wants you to have an eternal perspective on beauty, sports, food, not to rob you of joy but actually increase a deeper joy. Anything that brings you joy which isn't sinful is ultimately rooted in God. Therefore, God wants you to celebrate your sports team for His glory. He wants you to enjoy a good meal for His glory. He wants these joys

2. Matt Chandler, *The Explicit Gospel*, p. 125. Crossway. Wheaton, Illinois (2012).

to move us to bask in His grace, even in the midst of our sin against Him.

However, He doesn't want these second-place, temporal joys taking the place of the ultimate joy that is found in God alone. And the truth is, we receive greater joy in various spheres of life when we look to our loving God as the giver of these gifts. Our danger is when the creation becomes the consumer of our thoughts and not the Creator. When we worship the creation this is not only idolatry but this is when we begin to trifle, to waste time. We are trifling because our lives are being consumed with the temporal rather than funnelling our thoughts about the temporal through the eternal perspective of the Creator of those gifts. See the difference.

When I think of my current job, youth ministry, I know many guys who spend hours upon hours playing video games. I truly think these games are a gift of God if stewarded wisely. But hours upon hours? There may be some contexts where this is okay, but if this is a regular occurrence it could be sinful. We must keep video games, social media, blogging and other trivial matters in their proper perspective. Too much time devoted to anything, other than God, is idolatry and trifling.

Evaluate your life

Let me challenge you to evaluate your life a bit more from an eternal perspective. What aspects of your life could be considered trivial? This will be a challenge. The reason it will be a challenge is because most of us don't consider too much of our own lives trivial. Think of it this way. Sins are always easier to spot in others. We focus on the speck in another's eye more than the plank in our own (Matt. 7:4). Therefore, we could easily explain how others waste their time and see what we do as of great importance.

So, how do we decide what is trivial and what isn't? Take a look at any of your daily activities and ask, what eternal impact does this have? Now, we must not be too extreme in this line of thinking because there are eternal aspects to things that may seem insignificant at first-blush. Picking on athletics again. Some may claim that a win or a loss for a certain team has no eternal impact, which is true for the most part. However, if on your son or daughter's sports team you've noticed they have consistently been overly-aggressive towards their opponents, this could open the door to a good discussion. *Sally or Bobby, I noticed you got angry in the second half. What happened?* And now you've shifted from a temporal game to a heart issue of eternal significance.

All of this is to say, don't get too extreme in either direction. Yes, much of our life has been filled with trivialities, but let's not swing the pendulum too far and say we must always be reading Scripture, singing hymns, and evangelizing to fight against trifling our life away. We are called to live life in the world and life is played out through ordinary events. I know this is easier said than done, but live out the ordinary in light of the extraordinary (eternal).

Life is too short and too great a gift to waste it on trivialities, so we must be careful. We must funnel all of our activities through the mind-set of the eternal. Therefore I am saying you most likely need to drop some activities, and now I'm suggesting that you say 'no' to some trivial things. However, guard from being extreme and removing yourself from the world. Start bringing some eternal perspective into the trivialities of life. God commands us to be in the world, but bring His Kingdom to reign in whatever sphere you are in.

One of my favorite Scriptures that hits on this idea of eternal perspective is Hebrews 11:24-26, which we have already looked at briefly in chapter 3. Notice how Moses' eyes were moved off the fleeting pleasures of the world because his mind was consumed by this idea of eternity. It's easy to read this and move on, but consider what Moses was giving up. Money, comfort, pleasure, happiness, popularity, recognition, ease. These are things all of us long for and few of us would forfeit. Let that convict you:

'By faith Moses, when he was grown up, refused to be called the son of Pharaoh's daughter, choosing rather to be mistreated with the people of God than to enjoy the fleeting pleasures of sin. He considered the reproach of

Christ greater wealth than the treasures of Egypt, for he was looking to the reward.' HEBREWS 11:24-26

TIME TO THINK

✳ How much of your calendar's events are filled with eternal things? Do you volunteer for any ministries in your church? If not, why? Do you open up your home to show hospitality to others? If not, why?

✳ How much of your calendar is filled with temporal things? Do pleasure and entertainment define your calendar? God wants us to enjoy creation, but not at the expense of activities with an eternal perspective. Does your calendar show an imbalance towards fleeting joys?

5 BUSYNESS: NO TIME FOR GOD

WITH all of the aforementioned ingredients in our days they begin to fill up quickly, which doesn't leave us with much time.

I've been doing youth work in various capacities for the past decade. A few years ago I was meeting with a dear student who I had been discipling consistently for a couple of years. Since I knew the student very well and we had spent much time together, I was pressing this student to be a more faithful reader of God's Word.

My encouragement was due to the fact that the Holy Spirit uses means to change us in the Christian life and one of those greatest means and blessings is the Word of God. Therefore, I wanted this student (who was leaving for college next year) to get into God's Word more and make it a habit.

The student's reply to me was, 'I don't have time to read the Bible.' Since I knew the student well, I challenged him on this statement and said, 'What do you mean you don't have time? What did you do today?' His reply was something like this, 'Well, I got up and got ready for school. I went to school all day and then went to extracurricular activity "A". Right after that, I went to extracurricular activity "B" until supper. Then I got a quick bite to eat and went to work until 10:30 p.m. After that I got home and did my homework until midnight and then I went to bed.'

My response was, 'If you were a Christian you would read until 1 a.m. … just kidding.' In all seriousness, my response was, 'You're exactly right! You don't have time to read your Bible.' Every second of his life was filled with stuff.

We don't have time for God

At this moment, my eyes were opened to a reality I have seen again and again among students and Christians in general. That reality is, we don't have time for God. People may bristle at that statement or disagree, but I think our lives prove that it's true. I know many students and families that really love the Lord, but they just don't have any time to give to Him. It's a sad reality.

Kevin DeYoung, in his book *Crazy Busy*, warns us by stating many of the dangers of busyness deal with our spiritual life:

'Busyness kills more Christians than bullets. How many sermons are stripped of their power by lavish dinner preparations and professional football? How many moments of pain are wasted because we never sat still long enough to learn from them? How many times of private and family worship have been crowded out by soccer and school projects? We need to guard our hearts. The seed of God's Word won't grow to fruitfulness without pruning for rest, quiet, and calm.'[1]

The difficulty with this issue is that much of our time is filled with good things. Yes there are plenty of us who spend time on worthless things, (and I'll get to that a bit later), but the real difficulty that requires discernment is saying 'No' to good things.

A friend of mine once said, 'Good is the enemy of great.' There are many good things that we have committed time, money, and energy to, but are they the greatest use of our time? Are they the best way we can be using the time God has given us?

When Satan came on the scene in Genesis 3, he was described as crafty. One of Satan's craftiest tricks is making good things bad. Going back to the conversation I had with that student, everything he was doing was 'good'. The extracurricular activities were good, the job was good and

---

1. Kevin DeYoung, *Crazy Busy: A (Mercifully) Short Book About a (Really) Big Problem*, p. 30. Crossway. Wheaton, Illinois (2013).

taught him responsibility. But it's easy to see when you cram too many good things into a limited amount of time they become bad, even sinful things. Yes you heard me correctly they become *sinful*. Think about it, he was unable to fit God into the schedule he had. I would say that's sinful.

God, in His infinite wisdom, ordained, commanded, decreed that every day of our lives contain twenty-four hours. There is no way to change or alter this. Whether you are an atheist, agnostic, believer, or Oprah, this reality cannot be changed. This has many implications, but one of them is the reality that we must say 'no'.

Just say 'no'

There are many good things that we must start saying 'no' to. For example, at my church we have many different ministries. Some of those ministries are: adoption ministry, a special needs ministry, a youth ministry, an English as a second language ministry, and a church choir. I think it's safe to say that these are God-honoring things. However, if anyone decided to volunteer for every one of these ministries, that would be just plain irresponsible and foolish.

For starters, many of these ministries overlap, they each require a certain amount of time and God has only given you a specific amount of time in each day. Therefore, He doesn't want you to be involved in every one of these ministries. You would actually do a poor job at these ministries if you were involved in every one.

You see, the very fact that God has given us a limited amount of time in each day is a grace from Him. It is gracious of Him, because He wants to help you say no. We hate to say no for many reasons; we're people-pleasers and self-righteous. However, God is saying, 'I have given you these twenty-four hours as a guideline for the use of your time.' Therefore, honor the Lord, be faithful with the time He has given you, and glorify Him by saying 'no'.

Now I know that a blanket exhortation to say 'no' will not help anyone. Discernment is the difficulty here and I hope this book assists you to that end. Suffice it to say for now, start by looking at some things you could say 'no' to. The ensuing chapters will assist you with some specifics, but I'm asking you to simply accept the *truth* that you most likely aren't saying 'no' enough. In my experience, people say 'no' to church more easily than the world. The world often enforces punishment if you tell it 'no', but the church just gets labeled as ungracious or judgmental if they attempt to challenge in this regard. These are realities we must consider as we move forward.

TIME TO THINK

* Look at your life and see. Do you say 'no'? Why or why not? What things are you quick to say 'no' to?

* Are you too busy to include God in your day? How can you fill the time you have freed up by saying 'no' with time for God?

6 THE MUNDANE

I KNOW we've all coveted before. More specifically, at least for me, I've looked at the lives of celebrities and thought, *Man, it sure would be nice to be them*. We can easily look at them and think they have a life that is filled with comfort. A life that has so many luxuries; luxuries which seem to enable them somehow to avoid the curse of the fall. However, I realize that owning three houses and eating at every fancy restaurant gets stale after a while.

For example, I think we would be surprised to witness George Clooney's life for a day. I'm sure it's exciting and I'm sure we'd be shocked to see all that he has access to. But I'm sure we'd be shocked to see how ordinary his life might be. Of course, his life may also be so luxurious that he may long for an ordinary day, I don't know.

The point is, whether you're the Queen of England or an employee at Dairy Queen, all of our days are made up of quite ordinary moments. We get up, we tie our shoes, we brush our teeth, we go to work, we go home, we spend time with the family, we go to bed. That's just the norm. Of course, we have those extraordinary moments of tragedy and excitement, but that's what makes them *extra*ordinary.

As Paul David Tripp reflects on the incredible opportunities we have to parent our children, listen to what he says about the ordinary, 'None of us lives constantly in the grand moments of significant decision; there aren't many of them in life. No, we live in the world of the incredibly mundane.'[1] And if this is where we spend the most significant chunks of life, we better not waste them. If we are living for these *grand moments*, as Tripp calls them, we will miss out on our lives.

When we think of the apostle Paul exhorting us to *'keep a close watch on yourself and on the teaching …'* (1 Tim. 4:16) we realize the close connection between the theology we profess to believe and the theology we live out. Paul is telling us that we are all theologians and we may believe certain things to be true but the way in which we live may either affirm or contradict that belief. And these affirmations or contradictions are lived out in the mundane and ordinary events of life. Days which seem to simply blend into each

1. Paul David Tripp, *Age of Opportunity*, p. 22. P&R Publishing. Phillipsburg, New Jersey (2001).

other are actually amazing ways to profess the theology we cling to.

Our days are made up of numerous mundane moments which end up establishing patterns of great significance. God uses these mundane occurrences to conform us more into the image of His Son. A traffic jam, being left on hold, the paper jam in the copier, or the difficult person in the office, are used by God to make us more like Jesus. Ordinary, insignificant moments which make us more like the Second Person of the Trinity! That's anything, but ordinary.

A significant life

Every human being is made in God's image and is vastly significant because of that. However, sometimes human beings can long to establish their significance and they do so by trying to do something important. Men typically want to be admired by their colleagues, whether that's in the office, on the athletic field or in education. They want to be recognized. Women, too, want to show the world they are significant whether that's excelling over men in the workplace, being creative in the home and displaying said creativity on Pintrest, or attempting to be mother of the year. People are striving to be or do something important.

That's why we typically make war with the mundane. We want big, significant events to occur in our life. This is the appeal of Facebook. Facebook makes war with the mundane.

Instead of just tying your shoes, you can tell all 5,000 friends you just tied your shoes (you may lose some of these friends if you post your shoe-tying abilities). Facebook takes the ordinary and makes it extraordinary by allowing everyone to see it and 'like' it or comment on how others were tying their shoes at that same moment. It enables the mundane events of life to be lived out before an audience each day.

The reality is, someone else already lived a significant life for us so we don't have to and His name is Jesus Christ. Yes He purchased your life, so He doesn't want you to waste it. But you don't have to fight to make your life significant. He thought your life was significant enough to leave His throne and redeem you, because of the promise His Father made to Adam and Eve. Think back to God's promise in the Garden, which is known as the 'protoevangelium', the first pronouncement of the gospel (Gen. 3:15). God promises to crush the head of Satan and save his children, and He did that through His Son. His Son was cursed so that God's rebellious children would be saved from the curse (Gal. 3:13). Functioning under this knowledge of new-found significance, we strive after holiness in every-day moments. Realizing that our days are numbered, we don't want to miss out on these opportunities.

God uses the mundane to advance His Kingdom. Instead of being annoyed by the office gossip, you love them. Instead of snapping at your child when they ask for a candy bar in the grocery line, sit down with them and graciously explain why they can't. Instead of silently living in frustration with your roommate, you strive to deepen your relationship by talking about issues that are bothering you. Numbering our days helps us to see the significance of these moments. Both the office gossip, the persistent child, and the challenging roommate have eternal souls. One day they, as well as the rest of us, will live forever with the Lord or apart from Him, and this knowledge can give us grace to see these mundane moments as significant.

Seeing every day with new eyes

How many times have we heard tragic stories of familial relationships ending in fights? An angry father slams the front door in a rage as he speeds out of the driveway only to die in a car wreck. Or the rebellious teenager is tired of fighting with the parents, so she ends her life later that week. You see, the ordinary, day-to-day frustrations of life can drive people to do extraordinarily tragic things.

Numbering our days assists us to see that every conversation, every moment of laughter, every moment of frustration is a gracious gift from God. It may grate on your nerves that your teenager sloppily eats at the table at dinner-time by smacking or chewing with their mouth open, but one day that teenager is going to be out of your house for good. You may be intensely annoyed at your fellow co-worker, but God placed them in your life for a reason. Maybe you are the one the Lord will use to bring them to salvation. Maybe you are the only friend that person will ever have. Maybe the Lord is giving you a small taste of what it meant for Him to reach out to you.

While we may never make it in the world's eyes, every second of our day is highly significant. The last breath you just drew was a gracious gift from our Sovereign Lord. Any moment of difficulty is a blessing to experience. The fact that you have eyes to read this sentence, a mind to comprehend it, and fingers to turn the pages are all testimony to a loving God who gives us thousands of 'mundane' blessings every day. It's probably a good idea to stop and give Him thanks now …

TIME TO THINK

✳ How did this chapter redefine your view of the mundane?

✳ Do you see how significant little moments in life can be?

✳ How do you try to add significance to your life? Do you find yourself turning to social media to recreate yourself and attempt to validate your life?

SECTION 2

Biblical practices that assist our days

7 A WORD (OR TWO) ON STEWARDSHIP

WHEN I was in college I worked for a landscaping company. It was a tough job, but very rewarding. The owner, and boss, of the company was a very kind man and treated us in a laid-back fashion. One day one of my fellow workers was reflecting on a conversation he had with the boss.

My friend had worked for this company for several years and had gotten close with the owner. The two were reflecting on his years with the company and my friend commented on the fact that he used to show up late for work every day for quite some time. The boss, in a matter-of-fact nature, said something to the effect of, 'I remember that, I almost fired you.' My friend was surprised by this and said, 'You almost fired me! Why didn't you tell me?' The owner replied, 'You shouldn't have to tell an employee they need to be at work on time.'

What the boss was saying was the fact that there are some things that are just unspoken. There are some things a boss does not have to communicate to the employee; they should just know. Showing up for work on time is one of those. Likewise, a steward should just know they are supposed to care of something.

A steward is basically an employee who is put in charge of something. For example, if I were to pay someone to mow my lawn every Friday, I would expect them to mow my lawn every Friday. If they didn't care for it properly, cut it with divots in the ground, or if they didn't show up, they would be a bad steward. If they were a good steward, I would not have to call them and remind them to take care of the yard; they would just know they were supposed to do it.

Burk Parsons said, 'A "bad steward" is oxymoronic. A bad steward is no steward at all.'[1] So in reality there is no such thing as a bad steward. You are either a steward and you take care of what you've been called to do, or you are just a failure. But once you fail at stewarding, the title of steward is removed.

This idea of stewardship is asserted from the outset in God's holy Word. In Genesis 2:15 we read, *'The Lord God took the man and put him in the garden of Eden to work it and keep it.'* Think about this, Did God *really* need Adam to

---

1. Burk Parsons, *Not Lords but Stewards*. http://www.ligonier.org/blog/not-lords-stewards/ (last accessed: Sept. 20, 2015).

help care for His creation? God just created the universe by speaking! The reality is, He didn't even need to create Adam to begin with, but He did to display His glory. Now, God uses His creatures to care for His creation; i.e., stewardship.

Another helpful truth about stewardship is found when Joseph is testing his brothers in the book of Genesis.

'Then he [Joseph] commanded the steward of his house, "Fill the men's sacks with food, as much as they can carry, and put each man's money in the mouth of his sack, and put my cup, the silver cup, in the mouth of the sack of the youngest, with his money for the grain." And he [the steward] did as Joseph told him.' GENESIS 44:1-2

The steward is not *asked* to do something, the steward is *told* to do something. Reason being, the steward knew his place. The steward is inferior to the one in authority and God has called every Christian to be His stewards in various ways.

Christians often think of money when they think of stewardship. We think this because we must deal with money daily. Maybe it's because we've practiced poor stewardship in this area? We blow our money here and there and spend it on non-eternal things, but actually it's not *our* money to blow. As stewards, we are 'blowing' God's money.

Responsibility

In actuality, being a steward of our time is a far greater responsibility than stewarding our money. As I have already said, the richest man or woman on the earth cannot buy more time, which would make time more valuable than money. Therefore, to actually sit back and think about the reality of sitting in front of an infinite, holy God and giving an account for the ways in which we spent our time is quite sobering.

We are going to have to answer to the hours we slept, played games on our smartphones, talked on the phone, texted, watched TV or movies, surfed the web, blogged, gossiped, lied, and the list goes on and on. Broadly speaking, we are going to have to own up to the seconds, and hours, and days, and weeks, and months, and years we spent serving ourselves and our interests, above and beyond the interests of our Savior and others. Thank God He took on flesh and stewarded time perfectly to redeem our abuse of it.

The goal of this brief chapter is to understand that we do have a responsibility when it comes to stewarding our time. We live under the truth that the Lord has redeemed our time, but that faith should move us into action. We now must begin *doing* things to improve the use of our time. I know I've already asked you to say 'no' and begin to question the activities that make their way on your calendar, but we're going to move forward in this a bit and make sure you have some things on to your calendar. I have found that working with blocks of time (an hour or two) is helpful. Think of the greatest priorities in your daily life and block them out. This may assist you in stewarding your days.

We are shifting the focus from what Christ has done to what He expects His followers to do. We are called to live holy lives, which are uncommon from the rest of the world. Our actions should demonstrate to the world that we have been redeemed. Therefore, we must be active in ordering our lives in a way that brings God glory. This requires planning, scheduling, sitting down with a calendar, removing items from your plate and maintaining good stewardship.

TIME TO THINK

✳ How are you actively caring for the time God has given you? Are you proactively stewarding it? Talk to God about it.

✳ Do you allow events to come into your schedule without much thought? Do you find yourself saying 'Yes' with some frequency without thinking?

✳ What steps are you taking to keep from wasting your time? If you need help with this, it's probably a good idea to implement the '30-minute' experiment I mentioned at the beginning of the book. Keeping track in 30-minute increments for two weeks will reveal a lot to you. Why not try it out?

8 SABBATH REST

WHEN we begin to read the book of Genesis, we quickly see that there is a pattern in God's creation; that is, six days work, one rest. This pattern is something Christians often refer to as a *creational law*. This means it was something God established as a part of His creation, pre-fall. Since God established this pattern before sin entered the world, we tend to think this is an ideal way for Christians to try to live. If God, in His infinite wisdom, set this before us, it would probably be best if we heed His advice.

For example, no one in their right mind would tell Steve Jobs how to operate an iPod, because he *created* it. To a greater degree, God is the inventor of time. He is the only one who existed before time and is currently outside of time. Therefore, we would do well to listen to the Inventor who sets out a pattern for days of work and days of rest.

One can easily survey those in their local church and see that people are exhausted. Look at their countenance, their calendars, and their conversation and you can easily conclude that they are just plain zapped. I think a major factor stems from the fact that people aren't Sabbath-ing, or resting, the way God created them to. That is, the blessing of the Sabbath has become an unopened gift for many a Christian.

A question for you is, how much time do you spend thinking about the Lord's Day? Do you evaluate how well you are attempting to honor God on His day? Is Sunday a day that looks like every other day or is it a day you have set apart as God commanded you to? Is it a restful day you look forward to? While Christians view and define the Sabbath differently, in this chapter I will focus on the main truths about Sabbath rest that all Christians would do well to practice.

The Sabbath is a very sensitive issue to many Christians. We can be quick to accuse others of legalism or labeling them as judgmental when the issue is broached. In all honesty, Christians throw the word 'legalism' around way too often. Derek Thomas accurately communicates what many people mean when they throw around the word 'legalism'. He states that people often use this word when, 'obedience [is] inconvenient.'[1] Therefore, let's read this section with an open heart and mind and let's be cautious about using the 'L' word.

---

1. Derek Thomas, *How the Gospel Brings us All the Way Home*, p.49. Reformation Trust Publishing. Lake Mary, Florida, (2011).

Two truths Christians can agree on. First, God has placed importance on a Sabbath in the Scriptures. Second, our hearts are prone to wonder and are naturally at enmity with God and His Word. If our natural inclination is away from God and His Word, it will be natural for us to war against the intent of the Sabbath. What follows are some general statements which I trust most Christians would agree are good practice.

Preparing Your Body

You see, when we hear the fourth commandment we so often think that it is referring to Sunday. However, the fourth commandment initially calls us to think about every day, not just Sunday. The first word of the fourth commandment is 'remember'. 'Remember the Sabbath day, to keep it holy' (Exod. 20:8). The question for us is, what does it mean to remember?

In this case, remembering the Sabbath does not mean that when our alarm goes off on Sunday, our heads pop up from their pillows and we exclaim, 'It's the Sabbath! I remembered! I did what God commanded.' Remembering has a lot more to do with Monday through Saturday.

For example, if there is an athletic competition on a Friday or a standardized test for a student on a Saturday, the day *before*, the parent says something to the effect, 'You need to be home early tonight so you'll be at your best tomorrow.' The well-intentioned parent wants their child to receive plenty of rest so they'll have strength on the field or enough rest so their brain is fully functioning to remember all they've put into their cranium. *The days prior* to the actual event are used to maximize *the day* which is in focus.

If we know our children need to rest to be at their full potential in these other areas, doesn't this apply to Sunday mornings as well? I know that every individual needs varying amounts of rest for each day, so only you know how much you need, but has this idea of remembering been something you practice or model to others? The sad fact is that many Christians show up to church and are there only in presence.

As stated earlier, I work in youth ministry. And I hear plenty of students talk about being out until midnight or 1 a.m. or later (or earlier depending on how you look at it) on a Saturday night. Sure enough as I begin to teach Sunday school they close their eyes and get a much needed nap. The nap continues into the corporate worship as well. Some parents get frustrated at their teenagers for falling asleep, but my frustration is at the parents. What did you expect?! I don't care if George Whitfield was preaching; if I went to bed at 1 a.m., I would have a difficult time staying awake.

If you or your children are not properly remembering the Sabbath by getting enough sleep the night before, you are basically just going through the motions by showing up on Sunday.

While I firmly believe a curfew is needed on Saturday nights, I am not going to suggest you enforce that. Nor am I going to say this curfew should be strict, there are times when we have the freedom to stay up later. However, our Lord's Day worship is immensely impacted by the days prior. My challenge is that you pursue the Lord's Day the same way you spend time on your earthly pursuits. Start remembering the Sabbath the day before and make similar preparations for God's worship as you do for worldly pursuits. Let this be the constant day on your calendar that you plan around. Let everything else in the upcoming week revolve around this day.

Preparing Your Heart

'The service just didn't do much for me today … That sermon was just plain boring today.' These are some common statements uttered from congregants. Now, there can be much blame placed on the pastor for this, but there are other books to read for that and pastors definitely need to read those books and make sure they are being proper stewards of God's pulpit. But my question for the congregant is, did you spend any time preparing your heart for worship? [2]

Maybe the sermon wasn't boring at all. God's Word is anything but boring, so it could very well be you just weren't

---

2. One such resource that can assist congregants in listening to sermons is the booklet entitled, *Listen Up! A practical guide to listening to sermons* by: Christopher Ash, The Good Book Company. 2009.

paying attention or you've just gotten into the habit of showing up at church and wanting to be entertained. Yes I understand the preacher plays a significant part in this, but could it be that if you called on the Holy Spirit to help you pay attention, to get excited about His Word, to give the preacher boldness and passion, that your Sunday morning experience might have been a little different? Every congregant has the responsibility to prepare their heart as they come and gather with God's people.

How in the world should we expect to show up and hear from God's Word without praying? As I said, we are sinners who are inclined away from God and His Word. We are also in love with the things of this world. Therefore, if we aren't properly remembering the Sabbath by praying for our hearts, you can guarantee that church is going to be boring or that we won't get much out of the service. Don't you think God loves to answer prayers from His saints that ask, 'Please help me worship you today'? You better believe He does!

Preparing practically

Here are just a few more extremely practical tips that may help you remember the Sabbath. Obviously these are not necessarily Scriptural, but these are some things that help me to remember, or set apart, the Lord's day from every other day.

Even though I said these aren't necessarily biblical, I will start off with one that can be more easily applied from

Scripture. In Exodus 16, we read about God raining down manna from Heaven. As He explains what He is doing, He instructs His people to collect extra manna on the sixth day to prepare for the Sabbath. They were not to collect extra any other day, except the sixth day, because worms would destroy it (Exod. 16:20).

My practical application for this is simply prepare your lunch the day before so you can rest from slaving in the kitchen on Sunday. I'm not saying you're in sin if you prepare a meal on Sunday. But, why not use it as a day to rest from your daily routine? This helps you see the gift of rest the Sabbath was designed for, and it is also setting the day apart. Don't see this as a rigid law, see this as a gift.

For example, I love to grill out or barbeque. It's truly one of my favourite things to do. We typically grill on Saturdays and I throw some extra food on for lunch the following day in *preparation* for the Sabbath. After I'm done grilling, we put the extra in the refrigerator and we heat it up the next day. The meal is done and it is more restful on that day because of it. Again, not trying to be 'legalistic', but wouldn't this help you rest a bit more?

I know people vary on their views of going out to eat on Sundays, and I find that this routine assists us with this decision. It doesn't make lunch a chore on Sundays and it proves to be restful. Sometimes we even use paper plates on Sunday, not because doing the dishes is a sin on the

Sabbath but because it makes cleaning up that much easier and restful.

There are a few things we do differently to give our children some excitement about worshiping with God's people the next day. One very easy thing we do is simply pray the night before to prepare our hearts and to pray for the pastor preaching the Word. We pray that the pastor would get a good night's sleep and have boldness the next morning. We pray that God would begin preparing our hearts. This is an easy practice to establish.

We also say how exciting it is to *get to go* to the Lord's house to worship Him. We don't say we *have to go* to worship tomorrow. We are obviously honest with our children and let them know that sometimes we don't feel like going to church, but we need to pray that God would excite us about worshipping Him. One thing we do to foster excitement on the Lord's Day and help us remember this day, is we allow our kids to have sugary cereal on that day (sorry Sunday school teachers). Yes I know my children may only be excited about the cereal and not worship, but it sets the day apart and gets them excited about the Lord's Day. We tell our children that it's a day to celebrate Jesus Christ's life, death, and resurrection and one way we celebrate is by having special treats for our children on this day.

That's another thing we practice, simply referring to it as the Lord's Day. In my systematic theology class, Dr Derek

Thomas said something to the effect of, 'It's amazing how differently you will treat the Sabbath day, if you call it the Lord's Day.' This helps you remember it isn't your day to play golf or do what you want, it's the Lord's.

You may begin to laugh at a few of these suggestions, but I drink out of a different coffee mug on Sundays. Again, this isn't in Scripture and it's a bit silly, but it helps me remember as I'm setting out my mug the night before that tomorrow is a different day. I have discovered that this practice draws my mind to focus on worship the next day. God's Word is filled with visual reminders like the cross, the bread and the wine and this helps me remember that the day that follows is a different day.

We also lay our clothes out the night before, as well as our children's clothes. This is the only day I do this. It not only keeps us from being rushed on the morning of church, but it helps us remember that tomorrow is not like every other day.

We also don't turn on the television on Sunday morning. Watching television before church typically doesn't help you to focus on where you are going. If you do watch TV, does it assist your worship on Sunday? Does it set the day apart? For our family, the TV being off, assists us in both of those areas; i.e. preparing for worship and setting the day apart. I would strongly urge you to leave the TV off before church, this includes the internet as well. If you insist on watching, simply ask, how does it enhance your worship?

Getting up a little earlier to read and pray is also, I believe, a needed practice for each Christian as they go to worship. We really need to have a proper view of our sin and our Savior before we go to worship, therefore prayer and His Word are the means God has ordained to assist with this. We are at war against the world, our flesh and the devil; these are mighty weapons against this three-fold attack.

Often times we also play music before church. Either classical, instrumental, or hymn-style music to set the day apart. We rarely play music during the week, so this is another practical way to make this day different and remind us what we are about to participate in.

Silence and solitude; One blessing of the Sabbath

Not too long ago I read a tweet that said something to the effect of, *Because we're so busy, have so much activity, and are constantly on the go, this is proof that Satan knows how powerful silence is.* I wish I knew who said this in order to give them credit, but they are dead on. Satan knows the power of silence and reflection and has overly succeeded in making everyone so busy, that they have little to no time for reflection. Maybe you can't even remember the last time you had a moment of solitude?

The very fact that we actually have to make efforts to find solitude and reflection are evidence that Satan is hard at work to keep us from them. However, if that wasn't enough proof that the Christian must be seeking these moments, the Bible is clear on linking spiritual growth and our time of meditation.

Think of the verse *'Be still, and know that I am God'* (Ps. 46:10a). How many of you are being still? Being still will get you fired in this day and age. You must be on-the-go. Always moving in order to stay ahead. We fear that if we are pausing to reflect, others will think we're a bad mother, a lazy husband, or a slothful employee.

So much of our scurrying can be evidence that we don't believe in a Sovereign God. We feel that our work, our effort, our incessant schedules are going to accomplish what we need to get done.

Take time to find solitude. Find time to be still before the Lord. I know this goes against the grain of this culture, but moments of solitude are a must. How often do we see our Savior go off to be alone? Even when He's interrupted from moments of solitude, He still saw them as something He needed (Mark 6:30-34). We would do well to take pointers from the Son of God.

In Joe Coffey and Bob Bevington's book, *Red Like Blood*, they say the following:

> *'I am usually not good at solitude. I don't know many people who are. Problem is we are too used to noise. We have radios and TVs, laptops and cellphones and iWhatevers. Every once in a while I need to get away and*

find quiet. I have learned that quiet is something you must search for and when you finally chase it down it can be almost deafening.

Not too long ago I went outside to look for quiet. I found her by a stone wall. I just sat on the wall breathing and looking around and eventually I began to feel it. The ache. It is not exactly sadness but there is sadness in it. It is a longing. I think noise keeps people from feeling it. It is because of the ache that we can't even go for a walk without ear buds blasting distraction into our brains.'[3]

These moments of quiet reflection are powerful in God's hands. We are often reminded that things are not okay. The *ache* Joe speaks of is the reminder of life in a fallen world. We are so busy that forget about our fallen existence.

When we are still and quiet we begin to reflect on matters of great significance. We are reminded of who God is, who we are before Him and that our days are passing us by. We must be seeking and guarding days of quiet reflection, because they remind us of the fact that our days are numbered.

Again, this is a blessing God offers us in His gift of a Sabbath day. Even though much of our culture doesn't see Sunday as a different day, the pace of life is a bit different. For the most part, many offices and businesses are closed. It is already a day

3. Joe Coffey and Bob Bevington, *Red Like Blood*, p. 191. Shepherd Press. Wapwallopen, Pennsylvania (2011).

that's structured differently from weekdays; therefore let us use it to find solitude and rest. We think of necessities being food and shelter. Christ saw solitude as a *necessity* – do you?

A strong challenge for Christians: why the Sabbath isn't restful

Sundays have long changed from a day of rest to restlessness. Because extracurricular activities have made this day much like every other day of the week, with practices and games, parents are exhausted running all over the place. Homes are not peaceful and parents are running on empty carting their kids around everywhere. Maybe this is a day when you do all of your shopping? This is also something that often doesn't offer you the rest you need.

Many of these Sunday activities are a blessing from God, but they must be enjoyed in the proper context. When they abuse His day, this is not how they are to be enjoyed. In reference to extra-curricular activities, what we need are Christians who stand up with boldness to organizations and coaches and say, 'No. This is the Lord's Day.' If you had enough parents, or one parent who has a star player on the team say, 'We won't play on this day', things would change. Sadly, Christian parents are going right along with the rest of the world, treating this day like it was any other day. In this matter, we are *in* the world and *of* the world.

While on this subject, here's a thought to ponder. When we think of evangelism, Christians are right that sharing the gospel isn't the easiest task. We try to think of clever ways to insert it into the conversation or ways it could naturally be discussed. It's interesting to me that more Christians haven't seen the Sabbath as something to be utilized for evangelism. That is, if more Christians took up different practices on the Lord's Day, it would force the issue. Our unbelieving neighbors would inquire why we live differently on a certain day. This opens the door to the gospel.

When I run ...

Most Christians are familiar with the story of Eric Liddell. The Olympic gold medallist who refused to run on a Sunday. He was so emphatic about refusing to run on the Christian Sabbath that he stood up to the Prince of Wales himself. It's likely you are familiar with this story because it became a movie. The reason it became a movie? Because it was an intriguing story. And, it was not simply an intriguing story because Liddell could run fast. It was an intriguing story because he refused to run fast out of love for the One who made him to run fast. Christians applaud this story and rightly so, but then they choose a lifestyle the very opposite of this. Why be so moved by a story, but not live by the conviction that was being communicated?

I don't care if the coach says a prayer on the sideline or gives a little devotion, this doesn't honor the Lord in the way He wants us to. Just a few verses before this command to *remember the Sabbath* God told us that He is a jealous God

(Exod. 20:5). God has an extremely jealous passion for His glory and worship. Do you?

But don't see God as one opposed to your happiness. Don't think of the Sabbath as a day that locks you in your house, boring you to tears. Think about it this way; wouldn't you love a day when you didn't have to run your children anywhere? No games, no practices, just sitting at the house and resting from the busyness of the week? Guess what, God wants you to rest too. Use the Sabbath as a gift to rest. No rest and constant busyness leads to stress, exhaustion, sadness, and depression among other things. It wars against the way we were created to function.

You see, God is pretty smart. He knew where His creation was headed when He created it. He wasn't surprised that glory-hungry coaches and dads would want to have sporting events every day of their lives. He knew parents were going to be busy and exhausted because of activity. He knew we would desire to shop till we drop. This is why He created a day *as a gift for you* to take it easy (Mark 2:27). However, we have a history of thinking we are wiser than God and hating the good things He gives us. Therefore, take a step back, thank God for the good gift of the Sabbath and get some rest on this day.

TIME TO THINK

* What have been your practices on the Sabbath? Do you view it as any other day? Why or why not?

✳ What Scriptures shape your view of the Sabbath? Don't use your opinions, use God's Word. Has the world shaped your view of the Sabbath?

✳ Would you describe your Sabbath day as restful? If not, how can you make it more restful?

✳ Do you do anything to prepare for the Lord's Day? If not, why? Looking at the practical suggestions given to prepare for the Lord's Day, which do you think you might implement?

SECTION 3

Practically numbering your days

9 HOW MANY DAYS DO YOU HAVE LEFT? HOW TO ORDER THE TIME WE HAVE

DEATH is rarely a comfortable subject, but it's a reality that is set before us. According to the U.S. Census Bureau the 2020 projections for life expectancy for males are 77.1 and females are 81.9.[1] If you're in your thirties you've got around forty-five years left as a male and approximately fifty years as a female. If you're in your forties you've got around thirty-five years left as a male and approximately forty years left as a female.

Now, I know you can do math and the reality is you could die in a car wreck today; therefore these numbers are not facts we can base our lives on. You may live longer, you may not live to see your next birthday.

---

1. http://www.census.gov/compendia/statab/2012/tables/12s0104.pdf

So how many days do you have left?

Whether it's one day or one thousand, Scripture affirms we must be living with a sense of urgency. Listen again to what James says,

'Come now, you who say, "Today or tomorrow we will go into such and such a town and spend a year there and trade and make a profit" – yet you do not know what tomorrow will bring. What is your life? For you are a mist that appears for a little time and then vanishes. Instead you ought to say, "If the Lord wills, we will live and do this or that".' JAMES 4:13-15

James reminds us of a few things. First, it is our Sovereign Father, not you, who gets the final say. If He wants you to open the new business, He will allow it. If He wants your children to grow up and get married, He will bring that to pass. If the Lord is willing, it will happen.

Secondly, you are a mist. You don't have to know how to read Greek to see what is being communicated. Our lives are brief. Very brief. And we must be humbled by this reality. We must always have a 'Lord willing' mentality.

Therefore, as we are attempting to number our days, we should have a *mist*-mind-set at the forefront of our lives. A caution we must have from such a mind-set is to guard against anxiety. We must continue to make plans, we must continue to live our lives, and we must not live in fear.

A blessing we receive from such a mind-set is that our priorities should change. Since we know we are a mist and our lives are brief, it should change our focus. For example, if you knew you were going to die tomorrow your plans would be changed for that day. The decisions you made, things you once feared, cares that consumed your heart, would be drastically shaped.

Here's a personal example I've often reflected on. As I write this book, my eldest child is eight-years-old. As a family we try to plan one big vacation of the summer. If this remains constant, that means I have ten more summer trips before my daughter turns eighteen. That means if we don't miss any summer vacations (which is somewhat unlikely) I only have ten vacations before my daughter is out of our house. When she turns eighteen things will change drastically and she may or may not be in attendance at our family vacations. My days with my daughter are numbered.

This reality might depress some, but I think it assists me with a mist-mind-set. You see, we easily get lulled to sleep by the routineness of life that we can forget how precious it is. Having a numbered-day approach assists us in keeping focused.

Working within this mind-set, I have broken our days into three main categories; relational, vocational and recreational.

Relational

Scripture time and time again affirms the importance of relationships and community. We are created in the image of a triune God, therefore we long to be in relationship. However, which relationships are of greatest importance? Even though there are some grey areas in our relational priorities it is actually a bit easier than you might think.

First and foremost, our relationship to God comes before any other. If we are Christians and an eternity with God is before us, shouldn't we be developing that relationship now? If you don't want to deepen your relationship now, why would you want to spend an eternity with Him?

If your days are numbered, how can you best be spending those days to steward this relationship? Prayer and reading the Bible. Prayer is simply communication with God. Although that's a simple definition, it is not always a simple task. It is no doubt a discipline, but one worth working on. Not to worry, God is long-suffering in our stammering communication and the Spirit also aids us in what to say (Romans 8:26).

Not only are we to be praying, but we are also to be reading about our beautiful Savior. Since our days are numbered, we cannot be wasting them in worthless novels over and above the infinite Word of God. If you have never read the Bible cover-to-cover that is something you should strive to do before your days are over. If you have, focus on some books you don't know much about. Read some commentaries alongside them. You cannot exhaust the knowledge of God's Word, so pour over it time and again.

Even though God's Word should remain the primary literary tool for the Christian, there are many other Christian books that God can use to fill your soul. Since the time is ticking, ask your pastor which three Christian books were life-changing to him. There are classics every Christian should read before they die. John Calvin's *Institutes of the Christian Religion*, J.C. Ryle's *Holiness*, *The Confessions of St Augustine* and John Owen's Volume 6 on sin are some books that are a must and will add much wisdom, fervor and encouragement for the rest of your days. There are some other ideas at the end of the book.

Spending your days feeding this relationship will not be time wasted.

Our earthly relationships

If you are married, your spouse comes in second. How are you spending your time fostering your most important earthly relationship? In Justin Buzzard's book *Date Your Wife*,[2] he rightly claims that most men give up once they get married. They stop pursuing their wife. Men must be taking the lead in making the marriage an exciting relationship.

Plan weekly dates. This is something my wife and I try to do, even though at times we don't guard this like we should.

2. Justin Buzzard, *Date Your Wife*, pp. 53-54. Crossway. Wheaton, Illinois. 2012.

Personally, we don't have money to spend on babysitting and fancy restaurants, so we do date nights 'in' many times. We will feed the kids first, get them ready for bed, and then have a nice quiet meal or dessert by ourselves. We have found this one night to be quite refreshing. Couples need this uninterrupted time. We often try to come up with interesting topics to discuss, so our dialogue is a bit more meaningful. We may even eat in an uncommon room in our house to make it feel a little less routine.

Is there any surprise why the divorce rate is so high? Couples aren't taking the time to get to know and love their spouses more. If your spouse is to remain your standard of beauty, you must continue to get to know them. The more you know about them, the more you care about them and the more beautiful they become.

For those older couples, don't stop fighting for this relationship. Remember, your life is a mist. Do you really want the twilight of your marriage to be spent in front of the television? I don't care if you've been married for fifty years, you don't know all there is to know about your spouse. If you've been married that long, chances are you've forgotten a lot about your spouse - no offense.

If you have children, they all come in third place on the relational scale. Each year our youth ministry has a banquet for the graduating seniors and each year every parent exclaims how quickly the years go by. There hasn't been a year when parents aren't in sincere disbelief about the mist-like nature of their child's childhood.

Parents, you have such a brief time to influence your child for the Kingdom of God. As William P. Farley says, '[Parenting] is to transfer the baton of faith in Christ to the next generation.'[3] There is no doubt that God is sovereign over your child's soul and He does *all* the saving, but He uses parents to expand His Kingdom. His primary means of working is through the household.[4] Therefore, we must be spending time with our children. Praying with them, reading with them, evangelizing them, playing games with them, laughing with them, and discipling them because they will soon be gone.

Your church community is right behind, or alongside your familial relationships. Jesus Christ established the institution of the church, therefore, the people that populate your local congregation are vitally important relationships to establish and deepen. Scripture places emphasis on church relationships above others, as it says, *'as we have opportunity, let us do good to everyone, and especially to those who are of the household of faith'* (Gal. 6:10). While we know the family that shares our last name deserves specific responsibility, we must not minimize our brothers

---

3. William P. Farley, *Gospel-Powered Parenting*, p. 41. P&R Publishing. Phillipsburg, New Jersey (2009).

4. This thought originated from Farley's words.

and sisters in Christ. This is especially significant for those who are single in our congregations as well as the single mother or father who needs a helping hand. Think of what Christ says, *'"Who is my mother, and who are my brothers?" And stretching out his hand toward his disciples, he said, "Here are my mother and my brothers! For whoever does the will of my Father in heaven is my brother and sister and mother"'* (Matt. 12:48-50).

Look around

Lastly, and this is where the relational territory gets a bit unclear but hang on in there with me, I think the next relationship you should focus on is the one next to you. Look to your right and left. Your neighbors. You may say, *Wait a second! What about our parents? Extended family?* They may well be the next relationship on this spectrum, but I have no idea where you live in relationship to your parents. Maybe they are your next door neighbors. Chances are, most people don't live next door to their extended family, but everyone lives next door to someone, even if they are miles away.

Here's my point. God, in His infinite wisdom and sove-reignty, ordained that you live next door to the person you currently live next door to. Hmmm. If He has you living within feet or yards of each other, you don't have to think too intently to know He wants you to develop this relationship. That is why our neighbors come next. You may say, *but I love spending time with my family or my best friend*. That's great and good, but, if you are separated by states or many miles, God wants you to focus your efforts elsewhere. Think about it, proximity is what initially brought you close to your friends and family. That's why you like them. Now, however, if distance is what's in between you, God wants you to develop other relationships, it's not rocket science. And you shouldn't throw out the excuse that you don't have anything in common. You're both sinners who need Jesus, so start there.

One quick note about social media. I have discovered that people are reconnecting with high school friends through Facebook, for example. It is great and fun to rekindle these relationships we may have forgotten, but there is a danger here. One danger is distraction. You see, we were supposed to move on from high school, not continue to live in it. If you live in the same town with many of these high school people, then that's different. However, these old friendships can distract us from forming new ones with those next door to us or in our church community.

Being God's-image bearers, I think there's this desire to be omni-present and we try to remain close with everyone God has brought across our paths. We can't do it. I understand that we weren't ever designed to break fellowship, so there's a desire to remain connected to these friends that's rooted in the Garden, and social media seems to feed some of this mentality. My main point is to simply be a bit more discerning about investing too much time in relationships that are relegated to an 'online wall' like Facebook. There are many close friends I have on Facebook, but I must be cautious of investing too much in a relationship when others are physically present in my current life.

Vocational

People can often think of the negatives associated with work. These negatives include avoiding work, neglecting family for work, and working for the weekend. However, work was established pre-fall (see Gen. 2:15) and since we were created to work before sin entered the world, we will most likely be working in the new heaven and earth. Therefore, our vocations are good things that deserve appropriate investment of time.

Our vocations or callings are the specific ways in which God has gifted us, not to be successful, but to make His name known. Success may very well result in making His name known, but the world's definition of success and the Christian's aren't always the same.

Even though we recognize our relational calling to be superior to our vocational calling, we can easily reverse these. Tim Keller points to our culture as shaking its head at the child sacrifices of various cultures centuries ago, and we should shake our heads with disdain. However, are we guilty of the same? Many a father has laid their children on the altar in order to grow the business. Many a mother has sent their child to day-care so they could pursue a life of ease and comfort. I am not saying that day-care is sinful, but I am saying you need to search your heart on this one. The truth is, we sacrifice our children much more than we are willing to see.[5]

While numbering our days should drive us to pursue the vocational call the Lord has placed on our heart more fervently, we must be cautious that it doesn't subvert our primary call to relationship.

Living under the thought of this 'numbered-day' mentality, it should cause us to ask, *Am I using my gifts in my job?* God has given every human being unique gifts, therefore, He wants us to use them to point to Him. Are you doing that in your current job? Is your job simply a pay check? A way to take care of the bills?

There's nothing wrong with paying bills. Providing for your family is a good thing God expects (1 Tim. 5:8), but we must see more significance to the lives God has called us to. Our lives must be used to seek first God's Kingdom in all spheres of life.

Right out of college I took a job in insurance. It was a good job, I got great experience, and I truly loved the friendships I made at that job. However, some gifts others had affirmed in me weren't being exercised. I was definitely being used by the Lord, but not to extent the Lord wanted to use me.

---

5. Tim Keller, *Counterfeit Gods*, xii. Dutton. Strand, London (2009).

I realized, that I needed to move on. And this came to me on the morning commute. I was stuck in rush-hour traffic on my way to work, which was very typical of any day. As I was sitting in traffic I glanced at the car next to me. I noticed a young man, dressed in a coat and tie, headed to work. The cars in front of me moved forward, as did I, and I noticed an older man dressed in a coat and tie, headed to work. I had the thought, *That's me. That is going to be me. I am going to blink and it will be forty years in the future. I'm going to be older, dressed the same, headed to the same job.*

Let me first say that nothing's wrong with working the same job 40 years or more. In many ways that's admirable and displays perseverance and loyalty. Plus, we can honor the Lord in any job and the job you are currently in is the very job God has currently called you to. Therefore, I'm not trying to get anyone to quit their job and start living their life differently. I am, however, getting you to assess your life in light of these numbered days. Are you displaying the gifts God has placed in your life by your job? It is very true you can work your entire life and never truly exercise the unique gifts God has given you. There are many who never share their gifts with the Body of Christ. Is that you?

While I'm not trying to get you to quit your job, I am getting you to question it. Are you just in it for security? Money? Reputation/recognition? Ask people whom you trust to tell you your gifts. This could be your pastor, spouse or close friend. If your job isn't utilizing those, you may need to quit. But, you may need to stay in that same job and utilize your gifts in another context like church service or community service. You only have a certain number of days, so don't slack off in this search.

Recreational

Recreation is such a gift from God. Many of His graces are seen through recreation. There's a deeper sense of peace and freedom in our recreational pursuits, because they are *re*-creation. Our recreation is often reminiscent of creation, pre-fall. This is what recreation is supposed to be. It is designed to remind us of a simpler time. A time of peace and joy. A time that is free of life's burdens. But, we must be cautious of placing too much emphasis on our recreation. If our recreational pursuits become our only place of peace and comfort, instead of making us long for the new creation, they can quickly become idolatry.

Our lives are filled with recreation, but how much is too much? Do you really want to spend the limited amount of time you have on this earth in recreational pursuits? Some of you unhesitatingly might scream *Yes!* Some of us may think fishing off a boat, sitting on the seashore or traveling in an RV is the goal of life. And I understand that to an extent. By now, these words from John Piper are familiar to most and are relevant to reflect on at this point:

'I will tell you what a tragedy is. I will show you how to waste your life. Consider a story from the February 1998 edition of Reader's Digest, which tells about a couple who took early retirement from their jobs in the Northeast five years ago when he was fifty-nine and she was fifty-one. Now they live in Punta Gorda, Florida, where they cruise on their thirty-foot trawler, play softball and collect shells.

At first, when I read it I thought it might be a joke. A spoof on the American Dream. But it wasn't. Tragically, this was the dream: Come to the end of your life – your one and only precious, God-given life – and let the last great work of your life, before you give an account to your Creator, be this: playing softball and collecting shells.

Picture them before Christ at the great day of judgment: 'Look, Lord. See my shells.' That is a tragedy. And people today are spending billions of dollars to persuade you to embrace that tragic dream. Over against that, I put my protest: Don't buy it. Don't waste your life.'[6]

Piper's charge echoes the words of Jesus when He said, 'Whoever seeks to preserve his life will lose it' (Luke 17:33).

---

6. John Piper, *Don't Waste Your Life*, p. 45. Crossway. Wheaton, Illinois (2003).

Ultimately, if you spend your days pursuing life for *you*, you will waste it. So, how much recreation is enough? How many of our limited days should be spent in these pursuits? Here are some thoughts.

Christians aren't anti-recreation

Before we get into some cautions of recreations, let's look at some pro-recreational suggestions. Weekly forms of recreation with family and friends are excellent and God wants us to enjoy them. Walks around the neighborhood or on a nearby trail are excellent with family and friends and we should strive to have those moments. Bike rides and backyard sports are great and easy to do on a week-to-week basis.

As far as trips go, I think three-four weekend trips are excellent, but this will vary depending on the age and stage of life. These would typically be seasonal trips. Like camping in the fall, visiting family for Christmas, a spring break trip and a large summer vacation. Even though there is no strict biblical passage to grant a definitive number of vacation days, the Christian life is identified as one of work with rest and recreation mixed in. I think most Christians would agree that we can over-do it when it comes to too many vacations. Think back to creation, six days of work and one of rest. This does not mean there aren't periods of rest worked into our daily schedules, but there is work that needs to be done. Therefore, Christians need to be cautious of idolatrous pursuits of recreation. Are you vacationing too much? Going from trip to trip?

There are those who are imprisoned for the faith. Those who are being put to death for claiming the name of Christ. And while we shouldn't feel guilty that God has blessed us with a providence that allows us to vacation, let us not forget about those Christians suffering a more difficult providence in places across the world. Maybe we should forfeit a vacation from time to time in order to minister to those in need. While we need vacation and recreation honors God, we should also serve those in need (Phil. 2:4).

Many employers allot two to four weeks of vacation to their employees. Functioning out of this mind-set, here are some other suggestions.

Utilize the Sabbath

Since there's already an entire chapter on this, I'm not going to say much. But, if you are truly resting on the Sabbath, you will need much less vacation. Think about that. How many of you would love it if your boss gave you more vacation? I think most would say yes. Well, your main Employer, whose yoke is light (Matt. 11:30), does give you more vacation. If you truly use the Sabbath for rest, you would get over seven weeks of vacation, as I heard Pastor Ray Ortlund report on The Gospel

Coalition.[7] If you truly rest on the Sabbath, you will already feel less of a need to vacation. We worship a gracious God who gave us one day in seven to rest.

Utilize the weekend

The weekend is typically a time when we clock-out of the office, but punch-in as soccer coach, carpool driver, cheerleader, scout master, or any other activity we've gotten ourselves involved with. The weekend has become busier than the week if you consider the amount of activity that's crammed into fewer days.

But guess what? It doesn't have to be that way. Who's in control of your weekend? (If you said God, two points for the Sunday School answer.) You are in control of your weekend from the standpoint of what you're involved in. You can say no. You can relax at home. I'm not suggesting that you sit on the couch all weekend long eating potato chips, but slow down a bit. Do some chores around the house, do something with the family, but do *everything* at a slower pace.

Utilize down-time

The problem with the idea of 'down-time' stems from the question most of you asked when you saw the phrase, *what*

---

7. Ray Ortlund, Article: *Is the Sabbath Still Relevant?* http://www. thegospelcoalition.org/blogs/rayortlund/ ?s= is+the+Sabbath+ still+relevant (last accessed: Sept. 2015).

down-time? This is true, most of us don't seem to have down-time, but whose fault is that? We have filled our schedules with too many obligations, too many commitments, and too many things which are, quite literally, killing us.

The lack of down-time is running us ragged. The mother who is driving five kids in five different directions is driving herself beyond exhaustion. The father who's running his business, running in a marathon, and running his kids' soccer team is at risk of running away from a marriage, because he won't stop to give his spouse the time of day.

I've already suggested saying 'no' to many things, but let me add a caution here. Don't say 'no' to ministry. In order to guard down-time, I've noticed many people say 'no' to church in the name of 'family time' or 'rest' but they rarely say 'no' to the coach, the commitment to the team, or fun. Say no to the world, and yes to the church.

Just a helpful suggestion, pursue the sports or activities your child is gifted with. Listen, some of the more strenuous contact sports aren't for everyone. If your child continues to break bones season after season, it's pretty safe to say they were not gifted to play football or rugby. I'm not saying they shouldn't work through pain and trials, but there is wisdom in knowing some bodies weren't designed for this sort of punishment.

I know we've covered a plethora of topics in this chapter, so let me conclude. The reality is, at this moment, we have a certain number of days left that are ever-decreasing. We can't live in fear of this, rather trust in a Sovereign God who is ruling these remaining days. And, in light of this Sovereign God's control, live with a certain urgency by prioritizing those days. Look at your life in the categories of relational, vocational and recreational. Structure each of these days with the mind-set of *seeking first the Kingdom of God* (Matt. 6:33).

TIME TO THINK

✳ **What does this look like relationally?** Survey your relationships in order to prioritize them. Consider your various relationships and ask yourself, which one am I neglecting the most? Am I giving God the time I should? Am I neglecting my wife and kids? Have I ever talked to those people who sit on the second pew? Do I even know my neighbors' names? God ordains all the relationships in our path. Think of creative ways to invest in them and honor Him.

✳ **What does this look like vocationally?** Understand that God calls us and gifts each of us to work. What ways do you bring your work home? Do you find yourself checking emails incessantly on your phone? Do you frequently get up from the dinner table to answer your phone? Are you working harder to please those outside the home or inside?

✳ **What does this look like recreationally?** How do you plan your annual holidays? What time do you allocate to recreation and to ministry? Are you serving others at all?

10 TWENTY-FOUR HOURS AND NON-NEGOTIABLES

I'M going to be honest with you, I have never seen one episode of the hit television show *24*. I know it's probably awesome and I have heard everyone talk about it. I actually had a friend sit me down one time and tell me to be sure to carve out time for this show. One day I plan on watching it, but I need to make time first.

Although I haven't watched the show, I know the premise of the series. Each episode is in real time and an entire season is twenty-four hours. Not only does Jack stop bombs, viruses and assassination attempts, he can remind us of a reality we must all face. Whether we are a member of the L.A. Counter

Terrorist Unit or a stay at home mom, we all get twenty-four hours in one day.

Christians in the most practical way must look at the twenty-four hours in each day and begin to break up time in a discerning way for the glory of God. Remember, these twenty-four hours are God's helpful guidelines to us. Using this grace from the Lord, let's get really, ridiculously, practical.

I know this varies for each person but you need to go ahead and subtract six to eight hours from each day because we also know that God has ordained that we get sleep. Therefore, you're really working with sixteen to eighteen hours each day. Some of you have jobs which require at least eight hours, so go ahead and subtract that, which leaves you eight to ten hours.

This is where it gets a little tricky but we still have some direction. If you're married, you need to give time to your spouse. If you have children, you need to give time to them as well. However, how *much* time should you give to them?

To assist us with this, I think we need to break the remaining time into two categories; negotiables and non-negotiables. I think it will be helpful to start with the non-negotiables because these are issues that require time and are spelled out for us as a responsibility in Scripture. There will be some grey areas that require discernment but thinking about non-negotiables will help us along the way.

Non-negotiables

Prayer and the Word of God

One clear practice a Christian needs to make a part of their day is time with their Heavenly Father. If I loved my wife but never spent any time with her, she would have the right to question my love. Similarly, if we are not making any time to develop our relationship with God, one could question our love. I'm not saying you're not a Christian if you don't spend time with God. I'm not saying you must spend a certain amount of time with the Lord to be a Christian. And I'm not even saying you must make this a daily practice. What I am saying is that Christians should want to love God more each day. To truly love God, we must be talking with Him and reading about Him.

There may be some of you that question the fact that I don't say we need to read the Bible and pray every day. Why do I say *most* days? Well, life gets in the way and we will miss from time to time. If we are too rigid with an idea of a quiet time, we run the risk of being a Pharisee. I would argue that there are times that you would be in sin if you did read and pray at all costs. What?! Let me explain.

Most mornings I try to get up early to read the Bible and pray. Sometimes I don't, but I try to remain consistent.

There have been many mornings when I am reading the Word and one of my children begins to cry. Now if it's just a whimper I see if they will go back to sleep and sometimes they do. However, sometimes they don't go back to sleep and sometimes they begin with a scream and not a whimper. I believe I would be in sin if I thought, *Well, they're just going to have to suck it up! This is my time with God*. This could be sinful for many reasons. Maybe I'm being selfish with my time and my peace has become an idol. Maybe I want to shirk my responsibility as a father. Conversely, it could be a loving action to put down my Bible and help my child. Not only loving to them, but loving to let my wife get some more sleep while I care for the child.

So I'm not going to say you're in sin if you don't have a quiet time every day, but I would say you are most likely in sin if you don't ever do it. If you love someone, wouldn't you want to be with them? I know our flesh and our sin are working against us, but that's why you need to pray.

In Matt Perman's *What's Best Next?* getting up earlier in order to be more productive is advice he gives to everyone. He says that it affects everything.[1] This has proved to be helpful. There are times when it is difficult, times when I want to sleep in, but it has become such a regular practice I love it. And I find that it becomes less of a chore. I get up and try

---

1. Matt Perman, *What's Best Next?* p. 210. Zondervan, Grand Rapids, Michigan (2014).

to carve out time to be in prayer, reading the Bible, drinking great (strong) coffee, and sharing the time I have with the Giver of every second I've been given.

With the endless Scriptures given on the importance of being a lover of God's Word, I'll just pick one familiar passage.

> 'Blessed is the man who walks not in the counsel of the wicked, nor stands in the way of sinners, nor sits in the seat of scoffers; but his delight is in the law of the Lord, and on his law he meditates day and night.' PSALM 1:1-2

As I've said, sometimes life happens and you aren't able to get into the Word every day, but if you are consistently away from God's Word please do the following. Pray. Pray that He would begin to plant a desire in your heart. God in His infinite wisdom answers prayers in ways that are often different to our desires, but I tend to think He loves prayers of believers asking for a stronger devotion to Him. Pray those prayers and start carving out time. Start seeing this time of meditation as a non-negotiable. If you have to cut some negotiables out, do it.

Spousal Intimacy

I'm talking about communication … what were you thinking of? Working in ministry has shown me that spouses don't talk anymore. Yes they (sometimes) talk about their schedules, kiss each other good morning and good night, but they don't have long conversations. They don't sit and make time to talk about their struggles, temptations, joys, and vision for their marriage. They don't take time to work through their problems and disagreements. Often they ignore them and let them turn into bitterness. Communication takes time and communication between spouses is a must on our calendars.

What I have witnessed are husbands and wives that give too much time away to their children. Their children's activities dictate their week and drive everyone in opposite directions. When the spouses finally have the time to sit down together, they turn on the television or drift off to sleep. Rare is it, when husbands and wives get the chance to have lengthy, uninterrupted conversation.

As mentioned earlier, my wife and I attempt to have weekly dates. I think it's also a good practice to pick one night a week to read a theological book together. Husbands are expected to lead their wives and their household spiritually, so this is a practical way to follow that command. Again, I fail at this often and am convicted by it but it's something husbands must strive to do. What has been helpful is to think of your life in terms of semesters and pick a book you're going to work through as a couple for a semester. We don't do this in the summers because our schedules are pretty irregular and we don't do it during the Christmas holidays because of the same reason. Look at your schedule and plan accordingly.

We have much to work on in our marriage and we have our struggles, but these times have greatly assisted the joy, love and friendship in our marriage.

Now we get to the other aspect of intimacy. The one that's 'awkward' but shouldn't be. Husbands and wives must be making time to have sex with each other. Let's not make this uncomfortable. After all God commanded this (1 Cor. 7:1-5). This is the section on non-negotiables after all. If there are things God has explicitly laid out for us in Scripture we'd be doing well to heed that advice.

Think about it, many a sitcom has made fun of the fact that married couples stop having sex. Hmmm. Let's think about this for a minute. People who aren't married tend to have sex all the time with multiple partners, but then when sex is *ordained by God* in the context of marriage it stops.

Satan wants to ruin the gift of sex by getting people to do it in the wrong context, but then he gets you to stop when God wants you to do it. If you're too busy for this, stop doing some other things. I'm not going to give you a specific amount of time here. It should be enough for the Christian to realize that God has commanded this (isn't He so harsh?). Justin Buzzard gives some good thoughts on this in his book, *Date Your Wife*.[2] Without giving a specific number, let's just state the obvious

---

2. Justin Buzzard, *Date Your Wife* – this book is an easy read, so go ahead and check it out. You might not agree with everything, but I can almost guarantee it will help your marriage.

and say this must be happening during any given week. Of course I know some jobs separate husbands and wives for weeks at a time or people serving in the military are separated for even longer. This poses unique challenges, which is partially why God doesn't give us a hard and fast number.

Many Christians don't hold this Scriptural command with great importance. When they think of priorities, the husband and wife often don't factor this in. With the rise of porn addiction and divorce, I think couples would be doing well to heed God's advice. Just maybe this is *the* factor that has fed these other sins.

'For the wife does not have authority over her own body, but the husband does. Likewise the husband does not have authority over his own body, but the wife does. Do not deprive one another [of sex], except perhaps by agreement for a limited time, that you may devote yourselves to prayer; but then come together again, so that Satan may not tempt you [sexually] because of your lack of self-control.'
1 CORINTHIANS 7:4-5 (my clarification added in brackets)

In our busyness, husbands and wives are doing this less and less. If you are married let's simply believe that God knew what He was talking about here and follow His instruction. This shouldn't be a begrudging responsibility to follow.

Discipling Your Family

If you have children then reading the Bible and praying with them are practices that must also be occurring regularly. Family devotions are obviously a good thing, but I don't think you have to have them every day. That being said, there should be some formal reading and praying with your children that occurs throughout the week.

In Scripture, there seems to be much more emphasis placed on the informal discipling of your children. The Deuteronomy passage quoted below seems to imply the informal nature of discipleship that occurs when you *'walk by the way.'* This is why I don't think you *must* have a formal family devotion time every night. I do pray with my children almost every night. I read the Bible with them most nights, and I sing with them many nights as well. However, there are times when I share the gospel through everyday life at the dinner table. There are times when we color and I tell my daughter the muscles in her hands are a grace from God, so we should thank Him for that.

Many men shy away from devotions, because they think they're ill-equipped. When in fact if they were born men God has equipped and called them to lead even if it's hard. However, men must not feel like teaching Scriptural truths is a formal sit-down devotion. God is in all things and can be taught through the ordinary occurrences of life.

'You shall teach them [the commands of God] diligently to your children, and shall talk of them when you sit in your house, and when you walk by the way, and when you lie down, and when you rise.' DEUTERONOMY 6:7 (my comments in brackets)

This type of teaching is not necessarily formal. As I said, this type of teaching is done while driving down the road. Therefore, you may want to turn off the portable DVD and take out the earbuds and speak truth into your child's mind. These times are quickly passing you by.

Loving the Bride of Christ

Another non-negotiable is commitment to your church. Paul David Tripp says, 'I am persuaded that the church today has many more consumers than committed participants'.[3] That is, do you merely just show up on Sunday mornings and that's it? And, if you are showing up, how frequently do you? 'An active church member fifteen years ago attended church three times a week. Now it's three times a month.'[4] This should be a discouraging trend for all Christians.

---

3. Paul David Tripp, *Instruments in the Redeemer's Hands: People in Need of Change Helping People in Need of Change*. P&R Publishing, Phillipsburg, New Jersey (2002).

4. Thom S. Rainer, *Discouragement in Ministry*. http://thomrainer. com/2015/01/discouragement-ministry-rainer-leadership-086/ (last accessed: Sept. 20, 2015).

Service is a clear mark of a Christian. *'As each has received a gift, use it to serve one another, as good stewards of God's varied grace'* (1 Pet. 4:10). My question is, are you giving any of your time during the week to serving the church? If you only show up on Sundays, start by making time to serve your church in at least one other way during the week. This could be getting involved in a Bible study. I guarantee you that getting involved in a Bible study or prayer breakfast would greatly serve your church. It would encourage the one leading the study, it would encourage those in attendance, and it would also open the door to ministering in other people's lives.

Evangelism

It's interesting how many Christians seem to think that sharing the gospel is optional in life. I don't think any would come right out and say it but our lives display a lack of concern for people who are perishing. For Christians sharing the gospel is a must. This is not an option, but a clear command from Scripture. We must be telling others that Jesus Christ is the only way to salvation. Trust me, the 'Great Commission' from Jesus Christ is as convicting to me as it is to you (Matt. 28:19-20). I don't share the gospel with the passion and concern I should, but it is a command nonetheless.

I understand that there are many challenges to sharing the gospel and I want to be sensitive to those. Some people simply wonder, 'Where do I start? Should I go to the street corner and start preaching?' That's up to you, but I think the wisest and easiest place to start is next door.

Do you know your neighbors? Do you have them over? Are your neighbors Christians? This relationship was emphasized earlier, but reflect just a bit more. God created the entire cosmos. He flung stars and planets into orbit, ordained every earthly ruler into power and sustains every beating heart at this very moment. And God in His infinite wisdom ordained that you live next door to the people you live next door to. Was that by accident? A mistake? God wants you to get to know your neighbors.

These are the relationships you need to be focusing on. Yes the people in your church and other social circles, but I guarantee you that God wants you to invite these people over. You may say that they are strangers and I would say once you get to know them they will no longer be strangers. Plus, doesn't God's Word challenge us to show hospitality to strangers (Heb. 13:2)? When was the last time you entertained a stranger? Never?

In all of our prioritizing, we must make evangelism a key part and inviting our neighbors over is a good way to start. The house doesn't have to be immaculate and the food won't have to be five-star; all you need is the Gospel.

Exercise

There's no doubt we live in a culture that's a bit excessive about body-image. P-90X, Crossfit, Pilates, and yoga can quickly turn into idolatry that have, quite literally, formed bodies into graven images. Not to mention all the health and diet products at the local supermarket. Now I'm not saying that if you do any of the above mentioned forms of exercise, you're guilty of idolatry, but we must be careful.

Even with that caution, we must know that exercise is a biblical thing. The apostle Paul writes, '*bodily training is of some value*' (1 Tim. 4:8a). Paul is comparing bodily training to training for godliness. When the two are compared, there's no comparison. But he is not saying we shouldn't be training our bodies. Training our bodies, according to the above verse, does have *'some value'.*

If Jesus Christ purchased us on the cross, who are we to let our bodies waste away while on this earth? We should be cautious of what we eat and we should exercise. Remaining healthy only helps us spread His name to the ends of the earth. If we are obese and unhealthy, we won't be able to spread the word of Jesus Christ as effectively.

I want us to be very cautious when discussing exercise because we live in a culture that sinfully pursues body-image. But we must be a people who exercise. We were given physical bodies that must be doing physical things. Before the fall we were charged to work the ground; therefore we must expect to do some type of physical work quite often. Whether that's household chores, yard work or helping people move we will be doing physical working.

The difficulty with this issue is the frequency of working out. I think anywhere from three to five days would be good. Less than three probably doesn't help you that much, but I also think you could do more than five. As far as the length of time for each workout, this could easily vary. A twenty-minute workout is great for your body, don't feel like this has to be an hour. If you're a member of gym, I understand that you have to factor a commute in as well. Just know, you don't have to exercise an hour to steward the body like you should.

Even though the amount of time is difficult to determine I would say anything over an hour could be bad. I know there are cases where this could be fine but an hour is more than sufficient length to exercise. Maybe you're training for a marathon and you must run longer in order to do that. That may be okay, but the first question I would ask of the marathoner is, why? Why are you training for a marathon? For a 26.2 sticker on the back of your car? So you can show the world you've run a marathon? Maybe you're doing it for a personal goal. This is well and good, but running that much is a bit extreme and you must be cautious. What other things are you sacrificing in order to run 26.2 miles?

We exercise for health but often times this length of running does physical damage, so look at your heart on this issue.

For now let's just say, if your exercising time is taking away from the non-negotiables mentioned above, your exercise time needs to decrease a bit. That is, if your exercising is taking you away from reading of the Word, prayer, spousal intimacy, discipling family or serving the church, then you really need to stop looking at yourself in the mirror and take less time sweatin' to the oldies. If it's for a season, that's one thing. But if your exercise is consistently pulling you away from some of the aforementioned things, you should pause and think.

Interruptions

The story of *The Good Samaritan* is one that's familiar to most of us (Luke 10:25-37). The Samaritan was the only one who stopped and showed love to his enemy. He was the last one you thought would stop to help. Everyone else passed this man by, but the Samaritan went out of his way to care for this stranger. He spent a lot of money to love this man. The most significant thing the Samaritan spent though was his time.

Have you ever thought about this Samaritan's day? What do you think he had planned on doing that day? Was he supposed to meet someone or work for someone? He couldn't call them up and say he was going to be late. What obligations and personal benefits did he give up in order to serve this major inconvenience in his life?

Every one of you reading this book knows that interruptions are a part of daily life. Now we can't schedule interruptions and, if you do, they wouldn't really be interruptions. Interruptions are inconvenient and often annoying but we must welcome them to the glory of God.

The knock at the door, or the unexpected phone call, was ordained by God. Read that last sentence again. Every interruption was orchestrated by our all-knowing, all-loving Father. Again, we cannot schedule interruptions but must recognize them as a non-negotiable that will be a part of your day. Understanding this, you will cultivate a mindset that is more submissive to God's sovereign reign over your life.

The flip side of this coin is that there are times to guard from interruptions. For example, my family does not answer the phone during supper. That's one of the few times in our day that's guarded. I know we may get an emergency phone call, but God is sovereign over that and we trust in His providence. There are times we must guard from interruptions, so don't take every phone call. Pray for discernment here.

One Negotiable

Extra-curricular Activities

In some ways I want to list this category as a non-negotiable, but I've decided to list it here. Let me clarify a bit. We are clearly commanded to be in the world. Typically these extracurricular activities assist Christians to that end which tells me it should be something we make time for. The reason I've listed it as a negotiable is because you can be in the world in other ways.

When I list extra-curricular activities as negotiables, I'm referencing the time we allot to them, not the activity as a whole. In my experience, coaches dominate the amount of time we *must* give instead of parents telling the coaches how much time they will be able to give. I understand that parents realize that their child won't play if they don't abide by the coaches' guidelines. However, isn't it about time we challenged the culture in this aspect?

But many of these activities have not left us much of an option. The required time students and families are obligated to give leaves little to no time for God. Students and families are forced to choose God or a certain activity. This is not an exaggeration, I see this in student ministry first hand.

I know when football season begins, I won't see certain students for months. We can say that we love the Lord, we're about His Kingdom, and that we serve the church, but our decisions are modeling the opposite.

The solution is more parents and students putting their feet down and choosing the church over these activities. I know this is a challenge, I know coaches won't always understand, and I know you or your children will often feel the consequences, but we must get a handle on this.

Extra-curricular activities are often the major factor which hinders the spiritual growth of children. Let's give our children the opportunities to participate in the traveling drama club or excel musically with their voice, but start by telling the culture how much time they can have our children instead of the other way around.

TIME TO THINK

✳ The non-negotiables are in descending order in terms of relational importance; i.e., God, spouse, children, church, neighbors. What would you add to each of these categories? How could some of these thoughts be incorporated into your daily schedule?

✳ What are some negotiables that have been made into non-negotiables? What criteria are you using to define a 'negotiable' or 'non-negotiable'?

11 SOME NEEDED DISCIPLINES

AS I said in in chapter 1, the foundational truth of Jesus Christ redeeming our time for us has been the driving force behind my points in this book. If one were to lose sight of this we would quickly veer off into depression or works-righteousness and that wouldn't help anyone. Therefore, keep your eyes focused on the finished work of our Lord and Savior Jesus Christ. By faith in Him, you are righteous already. That being said, there are some needed disciplines you should strive for in your efforts to steward the days you have remaining. Here are some practical ways to assist you in your time-management.

Prayer

If you have a busy lifestyle right now and you are discouraged with the process of prioritizing, what makes you think you could be successful apart from the Holy Spirit? Most Christians are typically a little discouraged whenever they think of their prayer life. If we truly believe the Spirit is our strength we must bow the knee in humble reliance upon His strength.

But this isn't merely a general call to pray, here are some specific items to pray about. First, pray for conviction. We have wasted our time; none of us live perfect lives. Many days have passed us by. We have wasted time that was purchased by the blood of Jesus Christ. This is sin. This is sin before God that we must confess. Until you see your busyness as sin before God you will not be moved towards using it for God's glory.

Secondly, you must pray for wisdom and discernment. As we have said, many of the issues that create busyness in our lives are difficult to discern. What should we say 'no' to? What should we say 'yes' to? How much is too much? This is not easy. Therefore, ask God for wisdom in this area. We have already established the fact that you need to say 'no' to some things and you need to start saying 'yes' to other things, so ask the Lord for help. Wisdom is one thing we can ask for that God guarantees to grant (James 1:5).

Third, you need to be praying for discipline. Much of our busyness stems from the fact that we are not very disciplined. Much of what the Christian life calls us to is a disciplined life. Plus, many issues we have highlighted in this book call us to be disciplined. Start asking God for a disciplined life for His glory and His Kingdom.

Another issue to pray for is strength. The Christian life is a hard life. We are called to carry our cross daily and we will no doubt do this with our time. Pray that God would continue to give you strength in this fight.

And as you're praying in these various ways, don't forget to keep your eyes on the cross. You will forget the foundational truth, so go back to Jesus in your efforts.

Waking up early

For those of you who didn't skip over this discipline when you saw it in writing, I appreciate that. I know I spoke on waking up early, but let's have a little more thought on this. This must not be viewed as a hard and fast rule, but it is something that we must consider. Before we do so, please know that I am aware that there are certain jobs that call for crazy hours, so your job may keep you from doing this. I understand there are exceptions to this rule.

It is interesting how often Scripture talks about the morning or solitude. Jesus Christ, the Second Person of the Trinity, often woke up early (Mark 1:35). He sought solitude. He needed times of reflection. Yes both of these may be obtained at various times throughout the day but we all know the morning has fewer distractions. The phone doesn't ring. Blogs haven't been updated. No one is tweeting or updating statuses (for the most part). The world is quiet and God speaks to us in these quiet moments and we have space to speak to Him.

Pray that God will give you the strength to wake up early. If you are not a morning person and you could not fathom waking up early, two things. First, consider trying to wake up early for a season. The more you train yourself to get up earlier, the easier it becomes. It will take time to establish this habit but it is worth it. I used to be the biggest 'night owl' but am not much anymore. I don't miss the late nights. You ultimately cannot control what time you actually fall asleep, but you do have more control over when you wake up.

Secondly, if you have tried waking up early and can't establish the habit or your job does not allow it, find another time for solitude. A friend of mine does most of his devotion and study late at night. I know that Dr Albert Mohler, President of The Southern Baptist Theological Seminary, does his best work from 11:00 p.m. to 3 a.m. He states that it is during this time that he's 'most mentally alert and when [his] mental faculties are most available to [him].'[1] Reflection is vital to the Christian life. It is something you must work into your schedule. If it's early or late it's up to you, but you have got to schedule it.

Before we move on from the thought of waking up early or staying up late, let's have a word on laziness. Scripture has repeated warnings for the sluggard. Consider two proverbs: *'How long will you lie there, O sluggard? When will you arise from your sleep?' (6:9) 'As a door turns on its hinges, so does a sluggard*

---

1. Matt Perman, *What's Best Next?* p. 211. Zondervan. Grand Rapids, Michigan (2004).

on his bed (26:14). Again, sleep and rest are important and commanded in Scripture, but here are two verses that seem to have a negative view of sleep or the bed. If you refuse to get up early, it could be from laziness. It could be that you've turned sleep into an idol. This is something for you to consider.

We must be cautious of laziness. Work is a good thing, yet we live in a sinful world. Therefore, laziness will always be warring against our diligence. However, listen to this final exhortation from the book of Proverbs, *'The soul of the sluggard craves and gets nothing, while the soul of the diligent is richly supplied' (13:4)*. God rewards the diligent and the practice of waking up early says something about diligence.

Quality family time

Family time today often seems to be on the way out. Study after study seems to reveal that the family dinner table is being neglected. Yet, there are many reports that talk about how important it is for families to eat meals together.

One of the simplest, most practical and easiest (if you really plan) ways to have quality time is the dinner table. Our family has four to five dinners together a week. These are very important. It's important for me to be around the family God has given me and for me to give my full attention to my family.

It is very sad to me that families just aren't doing this much anymore. We know that we must eat to survive, therefore we need to make time to eat. But we must keep the family dinner table as part of the equation.

A point of application directed towards those who are married. Reach out to the singles in your congregation. Include them with your family. Consider their possible loneliness, especially around holidays. Make sure they know that they do have a family in Christ. Along with this, help the single mother working full-time trying to raise a teenage boy or the father trying to raise a girl. I am convicted over my blindness in this area, and pray that we'd have this 'family united in Christ' mind-set.

Guard social media

I think we are all aware of the great benefits that social media can offer us, so I'm going to jump right into the negative. They waste your time! All of the status updates, all of the pictures, all of the reading of the status updates. You look back at the clock and realize that you've wasted an hour. I have often been guilty of turning on the computer to do something entirely different and getting lost in social media. In many ways it's funny that I'm the one bringing this up, because I have been so undisciplined in this area at various times in my life.

If you wake up in the morning and the first thing you do is check statuses or tweet something, you probably need to back off a bit. Schedule times when you're going to check your accounts. This way you are more aware of how much of your life you're actually wasting on social media. Two things may prove to be helpful here. First, be intentional about what you're going to use social media for. That is don't simply aimlessly scroll through posts. Use it to contact a friend, encourage a friend, check some news. Second, deactivate your account. I've done this several times and it has proved to be beneficial. I think it's a practice most Christians should employ from time to time in order to resist being mastered by social media. It helps to take breaks from this online world.

Something else we need to cultivate is the fact that sharing something does not validate it. For some reason we think that sharing various aspects of our lives is only made worthwhile if we receive one hundred thumbs up. We think of something clever and we want to boast in our humor by tweeting it to our followers. Enjoy the life God has given you by remaining in the moment and not feeling a sense to share it with the world.

Something that could fit under this category is email. I am a person that checks email quite frequently and have become a slave to the inbox at various times in my life. Plan your email time. I think it's helpful and guards me from wasting time. If you are a person who perpetually feels the need to check your email, then take steps to guard against this.

Use a Timer

Doesn't the idea of a timer going off periodically throughout your day seem so appealing? I know this could be extreme but it can be very helpful and not as irritating as it may sound.

Earlier I spoke of the assignment I had in seminary where we had to log our day-to-day activity in thirty-minute increments. As challenging as that sounds it has left a lasting impression on me to this day. I did it for two weeks and it helped me develop a keen sense of time.

What I currently do is set a timer for my exercising and reading. I've found that it keeps me focused on the task at hand. Even if you have a timer on your watch that beeps once every hour, it causes you to be aware that time marches on even when our productivity doesn't.

TIME TO THINK

✴ What areas of your life are lacking discipline?

✴ When are you prone to laziness?

✴ What practical advice might you employ into your daily schedule?

✴ Remember, we are not validated by our hard work before the Lord. God does desire for His people to be a disciplined people. So don't beat yourself up over a lack of discipline, but take steps to start fighting against lazy habits that have crept into your routines. Confess and ask for strength to carry on.

12 GOD IS GOD AND YOU'RE NOT

A FILM I have watched many times is called *Cast Away* directed by Robert Zemeckis. It has excellent acting by Tom Hanks and deals with themes that haunt me still. It haunts me because it reminds me that God is in control of everything and often that means trial and affliction are just around the corner. It's haunting and reassuring. Reassuring because God grows us through affliction and trial; haunting because affliction is not fun and we would never choose it. If we would choose affliction then it would cease to be affliction, because by definition affliction is something we would naturally flee from. Confused? Back to *Cast Away* for clarification.

Affliction is something Tom Hanks' character, Chuck Nolan, quickly comes to be familiar with. His plane crash-lands on an island and he lives there all alone for around seven years.

As he gets back home, he finds out that life off the island has gone on without him and the reality is almost too much for him to bear. As he is reflecting on this reality with his friend, he mentions that the affliction he experienced was so severe it led him to the thought of suicide. He decided he would make a noose and throw himself off a cliff to put an end to his misery. Before he went through with his plan, he decided to have a test-run only to find out that the tree would not support his weight. He then exclaims, 'I couldn't even kill myself the way I wanted to. I had power over nothing.'

In reality most of us do not face trials to the severity that Chuck did. However, he conveys a truth that we come into contact with each and every day; we ultimately have power over nothing. God is the only One who is sovereignly reigning, not us.

To plan or not to plan?

I have lived long enough to be around people who don't know what they're going to be doing the next minute. They fly by the seat of their pants and go wherever the wind blows them. Perhaps these types of people won't even read this book because it's lying on the bottom of their trunk covered with laundry, a spare tire, a flashlight, and leftovers from their favourite restaurant they forgot were there. Most of these people read a few pages in this book and a few pages in that book, but they don't really plan to read a whole book because that would involve commitment. This obviously isn't the best way to go through life. To be honest, much of their life is wasted and it is poor stewardship before the Lord.

At the other end of the spectrum are the people that organize and plan to such a degree that it becomes idolatry. It is wise to plan weeks and months into the future and make commitments and say 'no' to things. However, sometimes people in this category forget to factor God into their plans. That is, they often forget that they can lay out their plans and be on top of things, but God is the only One who knows the future and His plan is the only one that cannot be thwarted. Our plans get thwarted each and every day.

Control freaks

This book is designed to help us reflect on the fact that our time is a gift from God and we are to steward the time that God gives us in a wise way. In order to keep from disgracing this call of stewardship, we must plan or else we may be in danger of being in sin with the way we use our time. However, we must also remember that God is God and we are not.

You could be the most organized person in the world headed to a lunch meeting with a very important guest, but something you didn't put down in your iCal was the car that just rear-ended you at the stop light. Or maybe you're the type of person that likes to arrive ten minutes early to everything. This can be a great habit, but do you scream and yell at your spouse and children when they are running late? It's great to teach your family good habits like being early, but if your 'teaching' is screaming and yelling, that may be a bad thing. It could be that the habit of arriving ten minutes early to everything has become a sinful idol in your heart and you have to know God always has you exactly where He wants you when He wants you.

There comes a point in time that we have to submit to God's providence. I'm not saying you have the power to thwart God's providence, but God gives us tests to grow us into the likeness of His Son. The traffic jam tests our patience, the late spouse or friend is teaching us to love even when it's difficult, interruptions remind us that life isn't about us. All of these moments sanctify us and give us opportunity for growth.

This idol of time is closely associated with those types of people we call *control freaks*. Often people who are more organized are organized for the sole purpose of attempting to control their life. They don't like surprises or the unexpected providence of God, so they attempt to plan, organize, and control things in such a way that they are in control of their own destiny. The caution for those who may struggle with being a control freak is starting by accepting the fact that you aren't in control. Just like Chuck from *Cast Away* couldn't control anything, you cannot either. But, be cautious because friends and family often become the brunt of your anger when things don't go according to plan. Be humble enough to see that the one you're really angry at is God.

Remember what James said,

> 'Come now, you who say, "Today or tomorrow we will go into such and such a town and spend a year there and trade and make a profit" – yet you do not know what tomorrow will bring. What is your life? For you are a mist that appears for a little time and then vanishes. Instead you ought to say, "If the Lord wills, we will live and do this or that." As it is, you boast in your arrogance. All such boasting is evil.' JAMES 4:13-16

There's a slice of humility for you! You are a vapor! Ouch, thanks James. He brings great perspective though. He's basically saying, 'Listen, plan as much as you want, but the Lord wills what He wants, not you.' Be cautious that you don't fall into the trap of being too controlling. Not only because it will frustrate your life less but you will honor the Lord and stop hurting all those who stand in your way.

Have patience

A song that my children have learned through the years is called *Have Patience*. I'm assuming that is its title, I couldn't find it on iTunes. It begins, *Have patience, have patience, don't be in such a hurry* … and just as soon as it begins, my patience goes out the window. In all seriousness, I think the song was designed to test your patience. This song does serve as a reminder however that I need to have patience.

Another sin that can rear its ugly head in those who make planning an idol is that of impatience. We all struggle with this sin in various ways, but I think most people don't realize what they are praying when they ask God for more patience. When the average person prays, *God, please give me more patience* or, *God, please help me not be an impatient person,* on the surface they are asking God for patience and are attempting to grow in this area. But what they are really saying is, *God, please don't ever allow any person or circumstance to come into my life that will test my patience. Remove all difficulties in my life!*

Most Christians just want frustrating, impatient circumstances to flee from our presence. This is understandable because we were created for a place of perfect harmony and peace. However, when you pray to God for more patience He hears something like, *God, I know I'm struggling with impatience, but I need to be a more patient person. Therefore, please bring about difficult circumstances and people in my life that will test my patience, in order to conform me into the likeness of your Son.* Only God's grace can help us to be patient people and when the difficulties of life come along we do need to pray for patience. But God often tests us in order to grow us.

To tempt someone is to have the hope that the person will fail and fall into temptation. To test someone, is to give them the opportunity to grow and succeed. This is what God is doing. If you are impatient and you ask for more patience God will, most likely, give you an opportunity to truly grow that patience through the difficulties of life. He's a loving Father that is for you and desires for you to grow into the full measure of His Son (Eph. 4:13).

The reality is, if God removed all of the annoying people or inconvenient circumstances in your life, you would not be more of a patient person at all. You would just have an easy life and would remain a controlling, impatient person. Plus, you'd be all alone because human beings are sinful and they would prove to be inconvenient to you.

If you are a fairly organized person, remind yourself that God is the one ruling and that, if you are His child, every annoying person and difficulty that comes along in life is ultimately for your good. God's sovereignty and providences are often mysterious to us, but He is the only One who existed before time and knows what the future holds. Not only that, but He took on inconvenience by coming to this earth. Peace, comfort, and ease were forfeited on your behalf. He did that out of love for you, so let that motivate you to hold a little more loosely to that schedule.

TIME TO THINK

✳ Would people say that you are an organized person? Why or why not?

✱ If you are a more scheduled/structured person, what are some ways this may be manifested as an idol?

✱ Do you find yourself angry at family and others, because of tardiness? Can you approach them about their tendencies to be late or is it something you need to take before the Lord?

✱ Does your scheduling show a lack of trust in God's sovereignty?

✱ Ponder the inconveniences Christ took on to walk this earth.

13 CONCLUSION

IF you don't mind, I will end on a bit of a personal note …

The writing of the introduction of this book to the conclusion has encompassed five years of my life. Don't misunderstand me, it did not take me five years to write this. For the most part, a draft of this book lay dormant for three years in my computer. Simply a Word document on a hard drive.

Much has changed over that time. My hair is a bit more grey, my family has added two more children (Jillian and Will), and I've begun the pursuit of a doctoral degree in youth and family ministry. Time marches on, as they say.

That being said, some things have remained the same. I'm still working in youth ministry, I'm still working in youth ministry in the same church, and I still love teaching youth.

Youth ministry shapes so much of my life, because my life is lived out in this ministry. And, it's my time around teenagers and their families that has shaped much of this book. I am often so encouraged and so ministered to by the lives of the students and families that are in my context. It's truly humbling. At times I am also a bit discouraged and concerned for the future of the church.

Not only are vast changes taking place and major difficulties presenting themselves at every bend in the road for the life of our teens, things don't seem to be slowing down either. Everything seems to be moving so fast and life is so busy that families rarely have time to address serious issues.

As I've read back over the manuscript, which now lies finished in your hand, I've cringed at some of the comments I've made. To be candid, I've been embarrassed at some of the things my younger self said. *Was I too harsh? How will people receive this particular statement? Am I going to lose friends over this? How will I be perceived?* I know I've said a lot in the preceding pages and have covered a lot of ground, which might have upset you. I pray, by God's grace, that God would use this crooked stick to make straight paths for His glorious Kingdom.

Even though much of what I've said may be misunderstood or, miscommunicated on my part, the conviction that drove me was the families in my church. The families in your church. Your own family. My own family. The family we all share in Christ and the lack of stewardship of time that is impacting them.

Busyness, trivialities, laziness, and neglect litter the paths we're all on. I am not writing to you as one who has the subject of *time* figured out. I'm writing to you as a fellow pilgrim. I'm one who fails at much I exhort you to and forgets to practice the very things I encourage you to do. However, if everyone waited to write a book until they've arrived, our libraries would be empty and our bookshelves lonely. I pray that I'll grow to practice much of what I've exhorted you to. I pray you do too.

Take time to rest. I know so many of you reading this book are exhausted. Take time to serve. Jesus came to serve and expects His followers to do the same. Take time to share meals as a family. Those children that make your house so noisy will soon be gone. Take time to open your home. Invite your neighbors and singles from your church into your home (just as our time isn't ours, neither are our homes … steward them well). Take time to be with your Savior. Don't neglect the time your Savior purchased with His blood by never stopping and thanking Him.

Life is so amazing and such a gift. We get one life to live and then an eternity after that. Eternity far outweighs the vaporous life you are currently living. It outweighs our life in terms of longevity, it outweighs it in terms of beauty, and it outweighs it in terms of fulfillment. We will one day stand face to face with the God of all creation. Let the awe of that Great Day shape your today.

APPENDIX 1
A CHARGE TO MEN

ONE of my favorite games I play with my oldest daughter is a game we call dinosaur. Basically we run all over the house and hide from a dinosaur that is walking around our home. We also use old cell phones, because people call us and let us know which room the dinosaur is in.

It really is a fun game and a special time for a father and daughter. However, I do have to say that sometimes it is a chore and it is the last thing I want to do. There is one sobering thought that often convinces me to play though. It is the fact that I will not always be able to play this game with my daughter. What I mean is this. My daughter is growing older each day and there will come a time when she is uninterested in playing dinosaur. One day she will become too cool. She will become more interested in clothes, talking on the phone, or chasing boys (not on my watch!) than playing dinosaur. And of course, she is supposed to outgrow those things.

The truth is, she must grow up. As much as I love her and enjoy playing childish games, if I am a good father I will be preparing her to leave me. But while she is in my house I must remember that each passing year with her is a gift, a gift that has a limited amount of time attached to it.

Because of our selfishness, I think fathers are tempted to see their wife and their kids as a burden. Sadly too many men are more interested in their golf swing or favorite television show than they are in discipling and loving their own family. This doesn't always mean that men don't love their families. It is because they get sucked into the temporal, trivial things of life and before they know it their children are adults.

One example the Lord has brought to mind again and again to help remind me of this reality, is a story that a seminary professor told my class. He was a senior pastor of a church and was actually dealing with this very issue of time. As he was discussing the difficulty of balancing church life with home life, I noticed that his voice grew weak. This sudden change in intonation grabbed my attention. The professor, fighting back tears, said that one day when his son was grown he said these words to him, *Dad, you robbed me of a childhood.*

The professor was educating us through his failure as a father. He had done what so many pastors do. They grew the church at the cost of their family. They cared more about what a bunch of strangers thought than those closest to them. This is something that happens gradually. A little more time on this sermon, one more hospital visit this week, one phone call that lasted a little longer, and before you know it, the time has passed you by.

Obviously this is not limited to the pastorate. The lawyer who takes on some extra responsibility to make partner, the business man who wants to make a little more money, and ten years later your children are in college.

One piece of advice for fathers; you don't check out when you get home. I know most of you, like me, are tired when you get home from work. Sometimes I literally lie on the floor in exhaustion and let my kids crawl on me to give them some form of interaction. But when you get home it isn't your time to rest and read the paper or watch highlights of the team you follow. Many men incorrectly and unbiblically think, *I've been working hard all day. I bring home the bacon. It's my right to sit down and have some peace and quiet.* I'm not saying you're in sin if you get home and read the paper or watch the television, but there are many men who are in sin and need to repent.

Chances are, when you get home, your wives are more exhausted than you are because they've been taking care of the kids all day or they work as well and are now working in the kitchen. Therefore, if you get home and it's 'your' time, you are not, as Paul says, *'Loving your wife as Christ loved the church'* (Eph. 5:25). Men, we must often die to ourselves and sacrifice what we want for the betterment of the family.

With each passing year, God has graciously revealed my sin of selfishness to me. And it wasn't until I got married and then had children that many selfish patterns were revealed to me. If you are not married or you do not have children, be preparing yourself now for these sacrifices. There are many times when I pray, as I'm literally driving into the garage, *God please give me strength to love my family and not 'check-out' when I walk in the door.*

A tough job

Men, we have a tough job. It's a tough job to be a husband and father, I know. I say it's a tough job because I fail at it every day of my life and you do too. If you don't think you do, you really need to get better acquainted with your sin.[1]

The great, encouraging reality of this impossible job is that both your successes and your failures point your family to Jesus. Anything good you do is rooted in grace so you get to point your family to Christ. And anything sinful you do shows where you come up short but Christ didn't. Therefore, let the good times and bad times point your family to Christ at all times.

The point is, you are to incarnate Christ; i.e. be Christ, to your wife and children on a daily basis. And you often can't incarnate Christ when you're sitting in the lazy boy

---

1. Obviously God's Word is the place to see mankind's sinfulness and develop a theology of sin, but here's one helpful sermon from John MacArthur entitled *The Sinner Neither Willing Nor Able*; http://t4g.org/media/2010/04/the-sinner-neither-able-nor-willing-the-doctrine-of-absolute-inability-session-iii/

sucked into the evening news. In all seriousness, what other news should be more important than what's happening in your living room? So what are some tangible ways we can incarnate Christ to our families?

Jesus Christ washed stinky feet

Every man struggles with pride in one way or another. This pride can manifest itself in the thought that we are above certain tasks or maybe some men think there are simply chores women should do and not them. And it is true that there are certain tasks that men do and women do, but if we are to engage in incarnational ministry with our families, we must often do pride-swallowing tasks.

Jesus was enthroned on high and left that throne to wash the feet of sinful men. So Jesus washed the feet of a bunch of misfits, traitors, and deniers. In fact, Jesus scrubbed caked-on faeces off the feet of His closest friends who were all about to run away and leave Him. As you know, there are no words I can type to convey to you the level of humility our Savior displayed through this amazing act of love. Our minds simply can't grasp this reality. We can reflect on it and we must reflect on it, but it's simply beyond us. Read Philippians 2 in order to get a better idea of Christ's humility.

Applying this to you men, there are times when you need to change diapers. You need to unload the dishwasher. You need to wash clothes. You need to take out the garbage. You need to turn off the television. You need to miss your favorite sports team's game. You need to tell your wife to go soak in a bath and let you bathe the kids.

I may not know you personally, but I know guys, and there isn't a guy on the planet who is above one of these tasks. The only Man who was above it was Jesus, but He got His hands dirty because He's the manliest man to walk the face of this earth!

Men, you must be taking time to serve your wife and your children and you must do that looking to Christ for strength. Every time you swallow your pride, every time you do an act of love like this, it helps you better understand your Savior.

For some of you this may be more difficult than others, but we all need the strength of the Spirit to do this. Therefore, every time you have to ask for strength, you are being conformed more to Christ's likeness and brought closer to Him through prayer.

Jesus Christ and children

Jesus Christ has been incorrectly portrayed in various ways by our culture. One misconception is that He was always polite. Don't mishear me, Jesus never sinned, but He did not always do what we would consider to be politically correct. He often called people out in their sin.

One unique example we see in Scripture of Jesus being 'impolite' was His rebuking of the disciples after they would not let the (less important) little children to Jesus. In Mark's account of Jesus and the little children, we read that Jesus was 'indignant' at the disciples (Mark 10:14). The Greek even says that this word most likely indicates anger that's physically manifested. It could very well be that Jesus was so angry He shook visibly.

I don't know about you, but if Jesus was so angry He was shaking, I wouldn't like to be around for it. There is no doubt that this was a terrifying instance but it is unique to think that it was in reference to the disciples' keeping little children from coming to Jesus. It wasn't dealing with abortion or rape or murder, but keeping little children from coming near Jesus. That might seem like a small offense to cause one of the only recorded instances of our Savior becoming mad.

One separate, but related, story we hear from Christ in reference to children is causing them to sin. He uses one of the most violently graphic images one could conjure up, by saying *'whoever causes one of these little ones who believe in me to sin, it would be better for him to have a great millstone fastened around his neck and to be drowned in the depth of the sea'* (Matt. 18:6).

Here's my point of application, men. Christ was clearly angry when the disciples kept children from Him and He conjured up a very violent image in reference to anyone causing children to sin. Are you guilty of either one of these?

Maybe you aren't stiff-arming your children from Jesus but are you making an effort to bring your children to Christ? Are you guilty of this by not doing what God has called you to do in discipling your children? Have you made the church a priority in your family's schedule or is Jesus (and His Church) what you go to if time permits? Are you reading your Bible to your children? Are you praying with them? Are you teaching them Scripture in the informal times of life?

It could very well be that you are in sin by not doing what God has commanded here. The above Scriptures are evidence that God is stressing the importance of this. In light of these texts, the truth cannot be overstated. If you take this lightly, it could very well be that you end up at the bottom of the abyss one day. Jesus' imagery here is intended to shock. However, Christ is not being shocking for the sake of shock, He wants men to wake up to this important truth and take our responsibility seriously.

There are many hobbies men take up; woodworking, tennis, golf, gardening, hunting, working on a car. The list goes on and on. Hobbies can be a good thing, as stated earlier. They can even be a God-honoring thing, something that God even uses to bring you into greater appreciation with Him. However, if God's given you a family, why not make them your 'hobby'?

When our lives are over, I doubt we'll wish we spent more time on the course or at the shop. I can imagine we'll want to spend our last waking hours looking at all those we poured our life into, knowing that they are forever changed by the love we imparted to them. And that they, in turn, will impart that love to the next generation. Although we'll know we fall way short of being a perfect husband and father, we'll know we relied on the power of the Spirit to live in a manner that reflected Christ.

APPENDIX 2
TEN GOOD CHRISTIAN BOOKS TO READ

Before I get to the list, let me just state how humorous this is. I never read a book until I got to college. Even while in college, I didn't read that much. The Lord worked on me and changed my heart in a mighty way to convince me of the importance of reading. As Christians, we must be reading because God has clearly shown us how important words are. For starters, He gave us a book. Secondly, He calls Himself the Living Word (John 1). Words are vitally important for Christians and while God's Word should remain the number one book in your library, God also gifted other saints before us with important words for the church. Here are some to check out, in no particular order:

Classics

1. John Owen's, *The Mortification of Sin*. This is adapted from Volume 6 of his works and I do list this one first,

because of its significant impact in my life. My oldest son bears the middle name 'Owen'.

2. John Calvin's *Institutes of the Christian Religion*. I say this with a confession, I have never read this from beginning to end. I have read most of volume 1 (books 1–2) and part of volume 2 (books 3–4). However, I plan to finish this before I die and many theologians I respect emphasize this work's continuous importance. It's often in the list of books people want if ever stranded on an island.

3. J.C. Ryle's *Holiness: Its Nature, Hindrances, Difficulties, and Roots*. My youngest son bears the middle name 'Ryle' if that tells you anything.

4. *St Augustine's Confessions*. One of the key works that has influenced many theologians.

5. *The Valley of Vision: A Collection of Puritan Prayers and Devotions*. It's hard to read this book without being moved. Some of the deepest, most thoughtful reflections of our great God and the love for His sinful children. It's a must own.

Modern

1. Paul David Tripp's *Instruments in the Redeemer's Hands: People in Need of Change Helping People in Need of*

Change. This book was ground-breaking in terms of a worldview for counselling. This book helped me to see that Christians are called to be counsellors in others' lives. Every Christian should read this; you won't be wasting your time.

2. William P. Farley's *Gospel-Powered Parenting: How the Gospel Shapes and Transforms Parenting*. This is the best parenting book … ever.

3. Kevin DeYoung's *The Hole in Our Holiness: Filling the Gap between Gospel Passion and the Pursuit of Godliness*. This book maintains a beautiful balance between grace and law. I think it's one of the clearest, concise and most helpful treatments on the Christian life; i.e. sanctification.

4. Tony Reinke's *Lit! A Christian Guide to Reading Books*. This is such an excellent book. It reminds the reader of why reading is important through a theology of reading. Then gives the reader numerous practical tips on reading. Any reader will benefit from this.

5. Tim Keller's *The Reason for God: Belief in an Age of Skepticism*. Confession number 2: I haven't read this. This has been on my 'to-read' list for years. Here's why I suggest it. First, I've read many other things by Keller and have been deeply impacted by them. Secondly,

many people I respect have spoken of the significance of his works. Because of his other books, his preaching, and endorsements, I'm sure this will be a classic among Christians.

FURTHER READING

WHAT follows are some of the works you may find helpful. Some of these I quoted throughout my book. While I only quote portions of some of them, most of what follows influenced *Your Days are Numbered*, in some way. You may find these helpful as they directly and indirectly deal with some of the content from this book.

※ Matt Perman, *What's Best Next: How the Gospel Transforms the Way You Get Things Done.* Zondervan, Grand Rapids, Michigan (2014).

※ Kevin DeYoung, *Crazy Busy: A (Mercifully) Short Book About a (Really) Big Problem.* Crossway. Wheaton, Illinois (2013).

※ Tim Keller, *Counterfeit Gods: The Empty Promises of Money, Sex, and Power, and the Only Hope that Matters.* Dutton. Strand, London (2009).

✴ Ted Kluck, *Household Gods: Freed from the Worship of Family to Delight in the Glory of God.* NavPress (2014).

✴ Edward T. Welch, *When People are Big and God is Small: Overcoming Peer Pressure, Codependency, and the Fear of Man.* P&R Publishing. Phillipsburg, New Jersey (2009).

✴ J.C. Ryle, *Practical Religion.* The Banner of Truth Trust. Carlisle, Pennsylvania (1998). Note: There are also free PDF's of some of these chapters online. I'm thinking of the chapters on prayer and Bible reading, which are priceless.